"Oh sing to the LORD a new song,
for He has done marvelous things!"

Psalm 98:1

I Have Set My King *on* Zion
Psalms of the Messiah

CONCORDIA PUBLISHING HOUSE · SAINT LOUIS

Copyright © 2008 Concordia Publishing House
3558 S. Jefferson Ave., St. Louis, MO 63118-3968
1-800-325-3040 • www.cph.org

By Jane L. Fryar, Jan Brunette, Suzanne Yelkin, Adriane Dorr, Diane Grebing, Rebekah Curtis, and Heather Melcher

Edited by Peggy Kuethe

Cover and interior illustrations © shutterstock.com

This publication may be available in braille, in large print, or on cassette tape for the visually impaired. Please allow 8 to 12 weeks for delivery. Write to Lutheran Blind Mission, 7550 Watson Rd., St. Louis, MO 63119-4409; call toll free 1-888-215-2455; or visit the Web site: www.blindmission.org.

1 2 3 4 5 6 7 8 9 10   17 16 15 14 13 12 11 10 09 08

a new song

I Have Set My King *on* Zion
Psalms of the Messiah

Meet the Authors

Jane L. Fryar enjoys serving God's people by writing and teaching. Her books include two titles focused on Servant Leadership, several LifeLight courses, the popular *Today's Light* devotional materials, and various other curriculums and resources for Christian teachers. Jane spends her spare time baking bread, lifting weights, and playing with Marty the Wonder Dog.

Jan Brunette's greatest passion is sharing the Savior's love through her speaking and writing. Her second passion is spending time with her extended family, now over fifty in number. In her free time, she enjoys craft painting, sewing, quilting, cross stitching, and traveling. A retired teacher, she still loves teaching Bible classes for women.

Suzanne Yelkin comes from a family of storytellers so it is natural for her to share her tales. As mother of four and grandmother of six, she thinks she deserves more gray hair. She and husband, Bud, realize that their descendants are every bit the sinners that they are and are comforted that God the Father's grace through His Son, Jesus Christ, is sufficient for all.

Adriane Dorr is currently enrolled in the deaconess program at Concordia Theological Seminary in Fort Wayne, Indiana, and spends her time working in both the Admission and Publication departments at the seminary and as the managing editor of *Higher Things* magazine.

Like the psalmist's heart in Psalm 45:1, the heart of writer **Diane Grebing** overflows as she shares the love of Jesus. "Because of their descriptions of God's constant care, love, and forgiveness, the psalms are my favorite part of Scripture," she says. For eighteen years, Diane has poured her heart into the writing of Vacation Bible School curriculum and LifeLight Bible study courses.

Rebekah Curtis is married to her favorite pastor. They live in Worden, Illinois, with their four children (to date) and one beast. Her de facto interests are breakfast, lunch, and supper, coming and going. She has an MA in exegetical theology from Concordia Seminary and, more important, makes really great pie crust.

Heather Melcher is a certified director of Christian education with a Bachelor of Arts degree in psychology and a Master of Parish Education degree. In addition to staying home full-time with her two young sons and occasionally helping her husband on their farm, she writes, presents workshops, and is developing a Christian resource Web site.

As for Me,
I have set My King
on Zion, My holy hill.
Psalm 2:6

Contents

How to Use This Book

A New Song: I Have Set My King on Zion is designed to help you grow in faith in your Savior, Jesus Christ, and to see how God works in your life as His precious and redeemed daughter. It is not meant to consume large blocks of your time. Rather, this book will help you to weave God's Word into your day. It will also encourage and uplift you in your personal and small-group study of His Word.

A New Song: I Have Set My King on Zion provides you and your group with six weeks of faith narratives based on biblical psalms. Each faith narrative was written by a real woman facing real-life issues—just like you. Each of our authors found help, encouragement, and direction for her life from God's Word and now shares her true story with you in her own words. Following each faith narrative, you will find questions that will encourage your own personal reflection and help bring forth meaningful and fruitful conversation in the comfort and security of your small group.

To derive the greatest benefit from your study, read the psalm in its entirety at the beginning of the week, and review it from time to time. Allow the authors' reflections on God's work in their lives to inspire your own. Write your thoughts and responses in the margins if you wish. Space is provided on the side of each page under the  symbol. Answer the daily questions as best fits your unique situation and the time available to you, but consider how your responses can further group discussion. The prayers offered at the end of each narrative will help you to focus on the weekly theme and emphasis as you respond to God for His gifts of grace. Use the prayers as they are written, or make them your own, changing and adding to them as they touch your heart.

Our prayer is that this book will enrich you as you look to our Savior, Jesus—God's Messiah and Holy King—in your study of His Holy Word.

—The Editor

Suggestions
for Small-Group Participants

1. Before you begin, spend some time in prayer, asking God to strengthen your faith through a study of His Word. The Scriptures were written so that we might believe in Jesus Christ and have life in His name (John 20:31).

2. Take some time before the meeting to look over the session, review the psalm, and answer the questions.

3. As a courtesy to others, arrive on time.

4. Be an active participant. The leader will guide the group's discussion, not give a lecture.

5. Avoid dominating the conversation by answering every question or by giving unnecessarily long answers. On the other hand, avoid the temptation to not share at all.

6. Treat anything shared in your group as confidential until you have asked for and received permission to share it outside of the group. Treat information about others outside of your group as confidential until you have asked for and received permission to share it with group members.

7. Some participants may be new to Bible study or new to the Christian faith. Help them feel welcomed and comfortable.

8. Affirm other participants when you can. If someone offers what you perceive to be a "wrong" answer, ask the Holy Spirit to guide her to seek the correct answer from God's Word.

9. Keep in mind that the questions are discussion starters. Don't be afraid to ask additional questions that relate to the topic. Don't get the group off track.

10. If you are comfortable doing so, volunteer now and then to pray at the beginning or end of the session.

Sane L. Tryar

Introduction

On July 7, 2007—that's 07/07/07 when written numerically—the New Open World Foundation announced the results of their attempt to name seven new "Wonders of the World." According to their Web site, one hundred million people from all across the globe voted via Internet and phone to select the seven new world wonders. The winners, in random order, were

* the Great Wall of China;
* the Taj Mahal in India;
* the statue Christ the Redeemer in Brazil;
* the Incan city of Machu Picchu in Peru;
* the Nabataean city of Petra in Jordan;
* the Colosseum in Rome; and
* the Mayan temple city of Chichen Itza in Mexico.

Marvels of engineering all, these wonders deserve a slot on everyone's list of "fifty places to see before I die." All except the *Christ the Redeemer* statue (completed in 1931) have stood for centuries; several of them have survived for a millennium or even two. Besides their beauty, all are marvels of engineering.

The more deeply archeologists study ancient cultures, the clearer it becomes that the technology of the ancients was in many ways no less sophisticated than our own. In fact, we today have no idea how their engineers did some of what they did. The procedural and technical knowledge has been lost to the human race; we cannot replicate their feats.

The World's Greatest Wonder

The latest Seven Wonders list follows in a long line of similar lists created from time to time since before Jesus' birth. The lists keep changing, in part because the wonders disappear. Those who voted in 2007 could not have included the Colossus of Rhodes or the Hanging Gardens of Babylon on their ballots, for example, because these landmarks have turned to dust and disappeared. Of the Seven Wonders of the Ancient World on most early lists, six have met a similar end. Only the Great Pyramid of Giza still stands—and it did not make it into the current top seven list.

Wonders come, and wonders go. Or so it seems.

This volume, the second in the A New Song series, focuses our attention on a site rarely nominated as a wonder. The faith narratives and Bible studies included here highlight Mount Zion and the King God has enthroned there. The title comes from

11

Psalm 2:6 and the words of our Lord as He describes the coming reign of His promised Messiah:

As for Me, I have set My King
on Zion, My holy hill.

The Lord could have chosen any place on earth as ground zero for the Messiah's ministry. He could have selected any thirty-three-year span in the history of our planet. Yet, He picked first-century Palestine. From a merely human standpoint, it was an odd choice.

We ask ourselves, "Could not God's promised Messiah-King have benefited in childhood and as a teen from the intellectual stimulation the great Library of Alexandria in Egypt would have provided?" We speculate about other potential alternatives, "Wouldn't the culture of a cosmopolitan city like Athens or the architecture of a world power like Babylon or the opulence of one of China's early dynasties have provided a more fitting throne room for the Ruler of the universe?"

But no. The Lord chose Zion—a smallish hill tucked in an unassuming corner of the Middle East during a time when the entire region lay pinned under the boot of Rome's brutal occupation. Many have written about the advantages God's choice provided, customarily pointing to the ease of travel Roman roads made possible and the advantages of Koine Greek, the language of trade then spoken across the Empire. Coupled with other details of history, both the roads and the language did, of course, make the missionary efforts of the first-century Church easier than they would have been at other points in the history of Abraham's descendants.

Still, *Zion*? Yes, Zion! And we need not rationalize the reasons. When we wonder why, our questions meet with several even more wonderfully foolish facts:

* God not only chose dusty, backwater Palestine as the earthly home for His Son, the world's Savior, He also chose us—you and me, rebels from the moment of our conception—to live forever under that Savior's gracious

Sane

12

rule. How foolish!

❋ By His sheer grace alone, He made us members of His Body, the Church—the eternal Zion. Another foolish enterprise, judging by worldly standards.

❋ And He chose to work forgiveness and salvation for us by the most foolish means of all—the cross!

❋ "For the word of the cross is folly to those who are perishing, but to us who are being saved it is the power of God. . . . For Jews demand signs and Greeks seek wisdom, but we preach Christ crucified, a stumbling block to Jews and folly to Gentiles, but to those who are called, both Jews and Greeks, Christ the power of God and the wisdom of God. For the foolishness of God is wiser than men, and the weakness of God is stronger than men." 1 Corinthians 1:18, 22–25.

Wonder-Filled Prophecies, Wondrous Fulfillment

The psalms you will study over the next six weeks shout the praises of Zion's King. They include some of Scripture's most powerful and prophetic words describing the Messiah's ministry on our behalf. The precision of the predictions you will read, most of them written nearly one thousand years before Jesus' birth, will take your breath away.

Even so, the wonder in these prophecies goes far beyond simple proof-texting. All, in their totality, call our attention to the tremendous sacrifice and overwhelming victory our King Jesus would win, has now indeed won, for us. All point to the Lord's wonderful love for us, love that led Him to His own death, love that now sends us as fools for Him to the ends of the earth to proclaim His resurrection victory to those who have not yet heard.

What wondrous love *is* this, O my soul!?

May the Spirit use the words in this volume and, especially, the wonder-filled Word of these psalms themselves to encourage and strengthen you in the true wisdom of our Messiah-King.

Week One

Psalm 2

[1] Why do the nations rage
and the peoples plot in vain?
[2] The kings of the earth set themselves,
and the rulers take counsel together,
against the LORD and against His Anointed, saying,
[3] "Let us burst Their bonds apart
and cast away Their cords from us."

[4] He who sits in the heavens laughs;
the Lord holds them in derision.
[5] Then He will speak to them in His wrath,
and terrify them in His fury, saying,
[6] "As for Me, I have set My King
on Zion, My holy hill."

[7] I will tell of the decree:
The LORD said to Me, "You are My Son;
today I have begotten You.
[8] Ask of Me, and I will make the nations Your heritage,
and the ends of the earth Your possession.
[9] You shall break them with a rod of iron
and dash them in pieces like a potter's vessel."

[10] Now therefore, O kings, be wise;
be warned, O rulers of the earth.
[11] Serve the LORD with fear,
and rejoice with trembling.
[12] Kiss the Son,
lest He be angry, and you perish in the way,
for His wrath is quickly kindled.
Blessed are all who take refuge in Him.

San Brunette

Psalm 2:1–3

Why do the nations rage and the peoples plot in vain? The kings of the earth set themselves, and the rulers take counsel together, against the Lord and against His Anointed, saying, "Let us burst Their bands apart and cast away Their cords from us."

An Unlikely Pair

No one could figure out how they could possibly work together. Angie was quiet, reserved, but very self-motivated. Her sister, Candice, was aggressive, outgoing, hated deskwork, but had incredible ideas. Angie stayed behind the scenes and wanted to remain anonymous;

Candice desired the limelight and craved attention. Yet, after their father's death, they decided to work together to improve the family business. Candice shared with Angie all the incredible plans that rumbled around in her head, excitedly met with the people needed to complete the tasks, and traveled to other locations to get the supplies required to finish the job. Angie attentively listened to Candice's plans and ideas, then methodically and meticulously carried them out, polishing them into perfection. They made a great team. In a matter of time, everyone discovered that the unlikely pair found common ground and used their skills and personality differences to accomplish their plan.

Unlikely relationships are common. Men and women who seem mismatched marry. Business professionals possess a variety of personalities and skills. The powerful become linked with those who are seemingly weak. Mothers and fathers are often more compatible with the child or children who are most unlike themselves. Sometimes, significant life events move the most unlikely persons to strive together toward a common goal. Yet, those relationships may not always be positive and wholesome. Hatred, envy, and jealousy also unite unlikely people and groups as well.

Many years ago, an Israelite king named Herod and a Roman ruler named Pilate joined forces to destroy a life. Two known enemies linked together to become friends (Luke 23:12). And all because of One who deserved neither punishment nor death. Too cowardly to resist the crowds, they ganged up and pronounced Him a criminal. One had Jesus ridiculed, mocked, and placed in an elegant robe. The other had Him brutally beaten and turned over to the Jewish chief priests, rulers, and people for crucifixion. Both played a part in His suffering and death but did so under the all-knowing eye of the Father who loved His Son, the Anointed One, and who had foreknowledge of this uncanny relationship before the world began. In the realm of eternity, both Father and Son not only knew it would happen but also approved its final outcome. The future of the human race was ever before them and, in their eyes, well worth the sacrifice. No amount of mere human planning could have laid a better foundation than

King Herod + Roman Ruler Pilate = distroying Jesus

Sam

17

was laid by Jesus Christ. No devising of murderous plots could alter the direction in which Jesus needed to go. No plots could slam the door for the salvation of the world, for Christ's love outweighed all the schemes and plans of men.

So what does all this have to do with me? I'm not working in business with anyone, like Angie and Candice are. Personally, I am not at war with any nation. I am settled in my own home, minding my own business, taking care of my own family. I was definitely not there when Jesus was before Pilate and Herod. The idea of those unlikely partners has little to do with me. How do those events of the Anointed One impact me today? Jesus' work of securing my salvation is done, completed, finished.

Because Jesus, the Anointed One, was willing to be hated, despised, and rejected, I am accepted. When that same Anointed One was buried in the grave, my sins were buried with Him, never to be brought to the Father's attention again.

Such were my thoughts as I studied Psalm 2:1–3. When asked to write about it, I wondered what my place was in all this. Yet, as I continued to study and write, I realized that through the person of Jesus Christ, it is as much about me as it was about Him. For you see, in the realm of eternity, when He endured the temptation in the Garden of Gethsemane, I was there. When ridiculed and abused in the presence of Herod, I was there. When Pilate had Jesus flogged and sentenced to death on the cross, I was there. When Jesus considered the uncanny friendship and the unlikely union, He willingly accepted the punishment out of love for me, keeping the joyful outcome ever before Him (Hebrews 12:1–3).

At one point in my life, when sitting in a pit of despair, I thought about Jesus on the cross and I wept. I realized that *my* sins put Him there. And yet, He endured excruciating pain and suffering on the cross *for me*. Knowing my sins were dumped on Him, I slowly began to realize that nothing—absolutely nothing— I could endure would ever compare to what He endured *for me*. What Jesus did was for the salvation of many—but also *for me*. On the cross, my debt was paid and cancelled in the eyes of the

Father. On the cross, I was redeemed and set free. On the cross, Jesus opened the windows of heaven *for me* so that I can now regularly communicate with my loving heavenly Father. Because Jesus, the Anointed One, was willing to be hated, despised, and rejected by men, I am accepted by my heavenly Father. When that same Anointed One was buried in the grave, my sins were buried with Him, never to be brought to the Father's attention again. Because of Jesus' resurrection, I am now free to serve Him out of love and dedication. He has given me the Holy Spirit as a sign and seal of His love and commitment to me. I am an heir of the Father, with an inheritance that will live throughout all eternity.

Today, the nations are still in uproar against the children of God. We view that all around us, not only in Iraq, Iran, and other places in our world, but in America as well. This was predicted in Revelation 12:17, where John states,

> *Then the dragon [Satan] became furious with the woman and went off to make war on the rest of her offspring, on those who keep the commandments of God and hold to the testimony of Jesus.*

Satan will continue to persecute us, but we know, just as with Pilate and Herod, nothing and no one reigns outside the loving shield and comfort of the heavenly Father. For just as He used the hatred and unlikely union of these two men to crucify Jesus, so He will continue to use the rulers of this age and their conniving to accomplish His ultimate, eternal plans for His people and nations. But we, as His children, will always be covered in the blood of Jesus Christ. He gives us the endurance, wisdom, and grace that only He can provide. No matter how much the nations rage and war against us, the comfort of the cross will always be our source of strength. It is written:

> *For your sake we are being killed all the day long; we are regarded as sheep to be slaughtered. No, in all these things we are more than conquerors through Him who loved us. For I am sure that neither death nor life, nor angels nor rulers, nor things present nor things to come, nor powers, nor height nor depth, nor*

San

19

anything else in all creation, will be able to separate us from the love of God in Christ Jesus our Lord. (Romans 8:36–39)

Prayer: Dear Father in heaven, because of the price that Jesus, Your Anointed One, was willing to pay, I can seek You with all my heart, pray to You at Your throne of grace, and willingly yield and offer myself to You as a living sacrifice. Through Your Holy Spirit, continue to grant me the grace, wisdom, and knowledge of Your love as I move forward in faith. Thank You for using everything in my life, both the positive and the negative, for Your glory and my eternal good. In Jesus' name I pray. **Amen.**

monday

Personal Study Questions:
Psalm 2:1–3

1. All the psalms in *A New Song: I Have Set My King on Zion* are messianic, that is, they focus on the Messiah—who He is and what He does for His people.

   a. What picture of the Messiah does Psalm 2, particularly verses 1–3, paint?

   b. How would you answer the psalm's opening question?

2. Read verse 3 again.

   a. What evidence can you cite to show that people today still repeat the rebellion described here?

   b. What light does today's faith narrative shine on that rebellion in our world?

   c. When have you participated in this rebellion?

   d. What will you say to your Messiah-King about that?

Psalm 2:4–6

He who sits in the heavens laughs; the Lord holds them in derision. Then He will speak to them in His wrath and terrify them in His fury, saying, "As for Me, I have set My King on Zion, My holy hill."

The Agony of De-Feet

The pool beckoned. With temperatures soaring near one hundred degrees, my four children and I jumped in and splashed around with great delight. Their laughter doubled my enjoyment.

My oldest daughter, Trina, relished splashing everyone around her. But on one such attempt, her laughter stopped abruptly and she emerged from the water holding her scraped and somewhat bloody foot. "Oh, the agony of de-feet!" she cried.

While I sensed her pain, I instantly broke out in uproarious laughter. Trina's ability to find humor in an unpleasant situation struck a chord within me. Within seconds, all of us, including Trina, joined in a chorus of giggles. What first was a moment of pain became in an instant a moment of joy!

This story occurred in the midst of one of the most heartbreaking times in our lives. My husband of seventeen years had just died at the young age of thirty-seven. I was left with four young children to support. Three weeks later, my father died as a result of a sudden heart attack. My children and I moved to a new home in a new location, and I began a new job. Life just didn't seem fair. I admit that at times I was angry with God. When others heard of my angry feelings, a few said, "Jan, you can't tell God you're angry!" My response: "Why? He knows of my anger anyway, and announcing it is cleansing and cathartic for me."

Pain is not something we want our children to endure. In fact, many parents will do whatever it takes to keep them from facing it. Yet life often takes twists and turns they cannot avoid— and we endure those difficult times along with them. Divorce, death, war, abuse.

It is comforting to know that God is a just God; He hates injustice. As a result, He is angry over sin and its horrible effects on people. He is angry with those mothers and fathers who physically and verbally abuse their children. He is angry with those who neglect their responsibilities as parents and instead follow their own greedy wants and desires. He is even angry at the nations, rulers, and others with power who conspire to wage war. He grieves as pain and heartbreak are needlessly imposed on us.

Yet, in the midst of all of it, His anger over injustice can point us to the King of Zion, who is truly just on behalf of all people. He reveals His righteousness even in the most unrighteous circumstances. Through His Holy Spirit, we can rejoice in the true Water of Life—God's Holy Word—into which we can plunge when the temperature of life gets too hot for us. In His Word, we are exposed to the cool, refreshing grace as it enfolds around us. We learn to bathe in His abundant goodness in the midst of the most churning,

San

splashing of times. And when the agony of de-feet seems unbearable, we have the One whose feet and hands were nail-pierced for us in injustice to make us just before God. Those same feet and hands guide and lead us as we swim through life.

We were not meant to flounder in this pool of life alone. We were not born to face the anger of our difficult times alone. We were not born to suffer needlessly alone. But we do suffer. However, in His Word, God reveals to us that He uses our suffering to polish and refine us, to conform us to the image of Jesus. Our Father desires that tragedies will turn our eyes to Christ, whom He has installed as King in the heavens. By His grace, trials make us more like Him. His Spirit uses our broken and contrite hearts to lead us to Christ and His ultimate sacrifice for us. On bended knee, we view the deep, gut-wrenching truth of the cross and the awesome power of the resurrection. With tear-filled eyes, our anger can turn into love as we see Him for who He is and what He has done for us. We love God's Word as the means His Spirit uses to feed our souls on a daily basis. We cherish our times in His presence, whether meditating upon Scripture and in prayer or in the Divine Service. We learn not just to love but to be in love with the Lover of our souls—the Savior of our lives, Jesus Christ.

When the agony of de-feet seems unbearable, we have the One whose feet and hands were nail-pierced for us to guide and lead us as we swim through life.

I can remember reading some portions of Scripture wondering how I could do the things He suggested. Sometimes I would get frustrated and angry at my own inability to do the things I knew He desired. For example, when Jesus said in Matthew 5:44, "Love your enemies," I would ask, "How? I can't do this on my own." When I read, "Do not be anxious about tomorrow, for tomorrow will be anxious for itself" (Matthew 6:34), I would again ask, "How? I have bills to pay and children to feed, and there just isn't enough money." When Scripture stated, "Walk in a manner worthy of the calling to which you have been called" (Ephesians 4:1), I again wondered how that was possible since I seemed to fail at every turn. Sometimes I wondered if God was angry with me because of my own lack of faith.

One night, all that changed. Awaking from deep sleep, I found myself crying over my own inadequacies. Then I remem-

Sam

bered Ephesians 1:17–18:

> *[I keep asking] that the God of our Lord Jesus Christ, the Father*
> *of glory, may give you a Spirit of wisdom and of revelation in the*
> *knowledge of Him, having the eyes of your hearts enlightened*
> *that you may know what is the hope to which He has called you,*
> *what are the riches of His glorious inheritance in the saints.*

Through that passage, God's Spirit revived me as I acknowledged His powerful love in my life. I understood that He was pleased, not angry with me. He loved me exactly as I was on that day, at that time. I realized the hard work of changing my inner being was the job of the Holy Spirit, not mine. The peace I encountered overwhelmed me as I cried and cried—only this time out of sheer joy. I knew I was loved and forgiven and *He* would do His mighty work in me.

As God is angry at injustice, so I need to be angry at injustice as well. But care must be taken lest my anger be because of my own self-pity and I lose control. Leaning on *His* goodness and strength in those times of temptation, I can surface the waters of anger without injuring those around me. Viewing others through the eyes of the King of Zion—who sees me redeemed and free—I can put others first, trusting Him to lead and guide me in His own gentle way.

Prayer: Dear Father, I often see life as unfair. When I see injustice on television, in the newspaper, or on the Web, I become angry. Yet I know You also are angry at injustice. I pray that You will give me the insight and discernment to know when that anger is appropriate and how to apply it correctly. Open my eyes to the hope that only You can give. Help me remember that Your Son, the King of Zion, still reigns forever on Your holy hill. Your justice in heaven will win over all injustice on earth. I pray this in the name of Jesus, who suffered the greatest injustice of all. Amen.

San

tuesday

Personal Study Questions:
Psalm 2:4–6

1. How does the Lord respond to the ravings of earth's puny rebels?

2. The words of the Lord in verse 6 terrify the rebellious. What makes these words so frightening to them?

3. Think about today's faith narrative and the author's comments about God's anger, injustice in our world, and our anger at God and at the world's injustice. What insights did all this open for you?

Psalm 2:7–9

I will tell of the decree: the Lord said to Me, "You are My Son; today I have begotten You. Ask of Me, and I will make the nations Your heritage, the ends of the earth Your possession. You shall break them with a rod of iron and dash them in pieces like a potter's vessel."

Feeling Unloved

Thirteen-year-old Brandy was stunned by her father's words. Although she had experienced his cruel tongue-lashings before, these words stung like sleet on a frozen afternoon. A proud young woman, she refused to show her pain and give her father the privilege of knowing how deeply he had hurt her. It was only later, in the privacy of her own bedroom, that she let the tears flow.

"Why, God?" Brandy cried. "Why would my dad be so mean to me? What have I done to be so unlovable in his eyes?

Satan wants to destroy the message of love, grace, and mercy offered to us by the heavenly Father. Using other individuals to fill our minds with his lies, Satan desires that we believe those lies rather than God's truths. While Christ grants us freedom— freedom from sin, from death, and from the devil's lies—we tend to bury God's truth of our eternal worth in the pillow of our own doubt. The heavenly Father is certainly grieved when His children believe untrue, negative words as they rehash them over and over in their minds, thereby undermining Christ's grace!

When I was growing up, I occasionally heard the phrase "Sticks and stones may break my bones, but words can never hurt me." Now that I am older, I realize how false that statement is. The more I hear from adults of the cutting and searing words spoken to them by loved ones—especially when they were children— the more I realize that the inner pain from words can last a lifetime. No matter how often others may affirm them of their worth and value, that small voice inside still wants to convince them that someone they loved thought otherwise.

Despite our faith, we can prefer to remain in the painful but strangely comfortable bondage of a dangerous self-image. Swallowed up by grief over what someone once said or did to us, our internal damage can often include a gaping hole of loneliness. We can refuse to see past the pain to discover the awesome power of Christ in our lives. We can prefer the familiarity of suffering to the freedom of our Savior. Eventually, believing the lies of Satan can feel more comfortable than believing the truth of God's Word. Yet Jesus is the Lover of our souls, and He desires and enables us to cross over from a painful past to a promise-filled future.

Many times in my life, when faced with put-downs or unkind words, I have mulled over them for days. However, when the Lord created in me a new awareness of His amazing love, I realized how important it is to choose to believe the truth of God's Word rather than Satan's lies. As the Holy Spirit has changed my self-image, I have discovered how amazing and beautiful is His peace that passes all understanding. Placing my thoughts in His care, by His grace I have been able to acknowledge that His acceptance of me was what I desired and appreciated the most.

Like our salvation, we have been given freedom from hurtful words and deeds by God's grace, which we receive through faith alone. Those who have been washed in the cleansing, forgiving flood of Baptism have been set free from all bondage. Because of Jesus, even in the midst of grief and pain, we find comfort. Even the gaping hole of loneliness is filled with His gracious love and promised presence. Enabling us to walk into God's presence through the door of Christ's blood, the Holy Spirit renews and restores our broken hearts and lives. He helps us acknowledge the pain, grief, and lies. He then transforms us into Christ's likeness and guides us to reflect on the Lord's grace rather than on our pain (2 Corinthians 3:17–18).

To understand the Father's great love for us, we need only look to Jesus, God's only Son. God proudly spoke about His love to His Son while He was on earth. At Christ's Baptism, the heavens opened and precious words from His Father echoed, "This is My beloved Son, with whom I am well pleased" (Matthew 3:17). At Christ's transfiguration, when Jesus' glory was revealed, the Father enveloped all those present in a bright cloud and announced, "This is My beloved Son, with whom I am well pleased; listen to Him" (Matthew 17:5)!

Desiring a love relationship with us as well, the Father continually views us, His beloved children, as redeemed, restored, and free because of the selfless sacrifice of His Son, Jesus Christ. Oh, the depth of God's love for us that we see in Christ's broken body and poured out blood on the cross! The love Jesus displayed on Calvary allows His Father, beloved from eternity, to cancel out our sins and wipe out the debt we owed to God because of them. In the process, God opened the door for us. With a deep abiding love, Jesus calls out, "You are Mine. You are precious in My sight and I love you. And to show that love, My Father and I opened the windows of heaven for you. I have cleansed you from anything that prevents you from experiencing the peace, power, and love only I can give you. My Father looks at you now and says, 'You are My beloved child, with you I am well pleased.'"

So what about the long-term effects of the painful words Brandy experienced from her father? While she occasionally feels a sense of inadequacy, as an adult, Brandy has forgiven her father. He died many years ago. While she still remembers her father's words, she does so now without anger or hatred. Rather, she understands and acknowledges hateful and hate-filled words as sins paid for by Christ. Now Brandy fixes her eyes on Jesus and her ears on what He says in His Word about her, not on what others say.

However, when the Lord created in me a new awareness of His amazing love, I realized how important it is to choose to believe the truth of God's Word rather than Satan's lies.

And what about us? Because of Jesus' cross, our heavenly Father continues to affirm us and forgive us as we stumble and struggle through life. Now risen and ascended into heaven, Jesus now rules and reigns over everything, also according to His flesh. Jesus' nail-scarred hands reach out to us daily, offering us eternal freedom in Him, not only in heaven but also today. The freedom He promises shines on others as we reflect His life and light. His Spirit's power is evident in the trials and tribulations of our lives. His abiding love enables us to love the unlovable—even those in our past who have said unkind things to us or about us. Acknowledging Him as our one and only source of strength in this life, we acknowledge that strength to be ours as well. Why? Because He is ours, and we are His—forever loved, forever forgiven, forever cherished.

Prayer: Dear Jesus, I thank and praise You that You opened the door of freedom for me. When the hurtful words of others begin to penetrate my thoughts, give me the strength to claim Your victory and acknowledge Your grace. Prepare my heart to receive Your forgiveness and to share that forgiveness with others. In Your name I pray. **Amen.**

Personal Study Questions:
Psalm 2:7–9

1. These verses quote the Father's words to the Son on the Son's coronation day.

   a. What does the Father decree?

   b. What does the Father promise?

   c. To what evidence can you point to show He has kept and will keep that promise?

2. What connections do you see between verse 8 and Matthew 28:18–20? between King Jesus and us, His royal priests, His holy nation? (See 1 Peter 2:9.)

3. When have the words of others hurt you, as they did Brandy in today's faith narrative, more deeply than "sticks and stones"? How could the insights you've gleaned from today's devotional time help you in similar future challenges?

Psalm 2:10–11

Now therefore, O kings, be wise; be warned,
O rulers of the earth. Serve the LORD
with fear and rejoice with trembling.

How Do You Fear and Yet Rejoice?

The weather had been incredibly beautiful and balmy. But within two days, everything changed. The sky grew dark. Black, angry-looking clouds rolled into view, an ominous sign of the horrible circumstances that were moving toward us. Overnight, the wind increased and howled through our back porch screen. In the morning, the rain began. At first it was a light shower; then the wind drove it so forcefully that it blew horizontal to the ground. Sometimes the wind died down a little; at other

times, it bent huge palm trees like plastic straws. Hour after hour, the rain pounded and the wind raged.

Suddenly, we were startled by a loud *thump*. Looking out at our neighbor's backyard, we saw that a huge live oak tree had crashed to the ground. More cracking limbs snapped around us, some landing on our workshop behind the house. Another crashed through a neighbor's screened porch. Everywhere we looked, debris covered the ground. As the wind raged and raged, we thought the storm would be endless. The lights flickered several times until the electricity finally went out. Our now darkened house was filled with the eerie sound of howling wind.

How could conditions change so quickly? One day the weather was bright and beautiful and all was well, and two days later a Florida hurricane changed the lives of many of my neighbors. Not only one hurricane left its mark the summer of 2005, but four hurricanes battered the Sunshine State and left buildings and beaches devastated.

Time has a way of alerting us to emotions never known before. Listening to the wind, seeing the rain, watching trees fall, and observing shingles and debris blow everywhere, I could not imagine how fear could be more real. Yet this fear was not just the fear of what I saw happening before me, but the apprehension of the unknown. However, as frightening as that day was, God's comfort and strength was evident then as well.

At night, during the height of that storm, I awakened to hear the whistling, howling wind. Shivering from fear of the unknown and unexpected, I was almost frozen in place. Realizing what this powerful emotion was doing to me, I prayed to God for strength and courage to face whatever might happen. Within minutes, the Lord brought a psalm I had memorized to mind:

Praise the Lord, O my soul. O Lord my God, You are very great! You are clothed with splendor and majesty, covering Yourself with light as with a garment, stretching out the heavens like a tent. He lays the beams of His chambers on the waters; He makes the clouds His chariot; He rides on the wings of the wind. Psalm 104:1–3

San

Repeating these verses over and over, I tried to envision God using those hurricane clouds as His chariot, riding on the wings of the very wind that was howling through my back porch screen. Within minutes, despite the glass doors rattling in my bedroom, an amazing calm covered me. I sensed an awe of His presence within and without. I realized I had *nothing* to fear, for I knew that the God who had the power to part the Red Sea, the God who calmed the Sea of Galilee, was also in full control of this hurricane. In the place of fear, I experienced awe and a godly fear and respect of who He was and how He would allow *nothing* to happen to me that was not part of His eternal plan for my salvation.

The God who had the power to part the Red Sea, the God who calmed the Sea of Galilee, was also in full control of this hurricane. . . . He would allow nothing to happen to me that was not part of His eternal plan for my salvation.

Recalling that summer and remembering those dark clouds that pummeled Florida and other southern states, I am reminded even more of the dark and frightening events that occurred on Calvary. Shrouded with ugliness—not only in nature, but also in the cruelly tortured and battered body of our Lord, Jesus Christ—God's incredible hatred of sin was exposed. That terrible fear of God's wrath was laid upon Jesus, yet His love endured it all for us. There He conquered sin, death, and the devil for us. Because of His sacrifice, we are free from the fear of God's righteous judgment as we receive what He freely gives by grace.

When I was growing up, I remember reading that I was to "fear" the Lord. The psalms referred to it in passage after passage. In confirmation class, I recited Luther's explanation to the Commandments, beginning with the words "We should fear and love God. . . ." At that time in my life, my understanding of fear was that of shivering in one's boots, terrified of impending doom. Psalm 2:11 only confirmed my impression: "Serve the LORD with fear, and rejoice with trembling." How could one connect fear and trembling with serving and rejoicing? We call that an oxymoron— a word or phrase that is seemingly opposite in meaning.

On resurrection day, Jesus announced that our sins were

buried and a new life in Him was made possible. What an incredible oxymoron—buried, yet alive! And as a result of that oxymoron, many more such experiences are possible. We can easily come up with several examples: we are poor in spirit, yet we possess the kingdom of God; we are mournful, yet we are comforted; we are meek, yet we will inherit the earth; we deny ourselves, yet we have gained an eternal inheritance; we fear God, yet we serve Him out of love; we tremble, yet we rejoice in Christ.

Realizing that on the cross God's awful, dreadful punishment of sin was replaced with His undeserved grace and mercy, I am learning to embrace the fearful, shivering times of my life with awe and respect. I seek to zealously serve God in His kingdom's work and rejoice that I am a part of it. Seeking Christ in His Word, I pray for His revelations of love and encouragement as I learn more of Him, of His will, and of His eternal desires for my life. Acknowledging that I am not only saved by His grace but am also His own workmanship, recreated in Christ to do good works, I pray for the strength to accomplish His purposes for me and for others, knowing that He prepared them in advance for me to do (Ephesians 2:8–10).

Given a heart of gratitude, a dedicated will to serve, and a hunger for Christ and His Word, I am learning to rejoice in all that He has given—not because I deserve it, but because He gave it to me out of love. Desiring to give God all the glory, I choose to serve Him with truly awesome fear and tremble with love and excitement for His sacrifice of love and His gift of forgiveness. Hurricanes come and hurricanes go. But as the psalmist says, even in their midst we can "serve the LORD with fear, and rejoice with trembling."

San

Prayer: Dear Jesus, I praise and thank You that You willingly remove my fear of judgment and replace it with a wonderful, loving respect of the Father. Redeemed and freed from sin's condemnation, give me the desire to serve You with respectful fear and rejoice with trembling excitement—a sign of my love to You. Grant me Your Holy Spirit as I learn to love You more and yearn to share that love with others. In Your name I pray. **Amen.**

thursday

Personal Study Questions:
Psalm 2:10–11

1. Psalm 2 describes the Messiah's royalty, rule, and wrath.

   a. To which of these three do verses 10–11 most closely connect? Explain.

   b. What warning do you see in verse 10?

   c. How does that warning fit in with Psalm 111:10?

2. To what oxymoron in 2:11 does today's faith narrative point? What creates the dynamic tension in that verse? How do you resolve this tension in your own heart?

Psalm 2:12

*Kiss the Son, lest He be angry and you
perish in the way, for His wrath is quickly kindled.
Blessed are all who take refuge in Him.*

Pheasant under Glass

As I stood and stared at the donuts behind the counter, I debated whether I should indulge. I love glazed donuts. They were in abundance that day, and my heart was especially craving the French crullers. For me, every bite of a cruller tastes like cream puffs—without the calories of the cream. When I heard the young lady's offer to assist me in my selection, I yielded to the temptation.

"I'll take one of those French crullers with chocolate frosting," I said with a smile. I believed the woman could sense my desire for this scrumptious dessert, so I couldn't resist telling her how I looked forward to eating it as my treat for the day.

Then, for some reason, she began sharing with me a story that had nothing to do with donuts. It had to do with her mother:

"I could tell something was different when I went into her bedroom. I wanted to do something really special for her and said, 'Mom, what would you like for dinner today? I will fix you anything you want. Just ask, and I will make it for you.' My mother gave me the sweetest look and replied, 'Pheasant under glass.' I was shocked as my mother had never eaten nor requested pheasant under glass before. Yet, within minutes after answering, she closed her eyes and died. I just can't imagine what motivated her to ask for it."

Without even a second thought, I responded, "Maybe that was what she was requesting at the banquet feast in heaven."

At first the woman seemed startled by my remark, but then appeared calm and said, "Maybe you're right. Maybe you're right."

With that, I took my French cruller and headed for the checkout counter. On the way, I thought about my remark and how it surprised me that I had said it. I thought, *What possessed me to say that? Thank You, Lord, for helping me think of it!* Returning to my car, I began eating the tasty pastry. Relishing every bite, I thought about the precious woman who, in a sense, might be enjoying "pheasant under glass" with Jesus.

I grew up at a time when pheasant under glass was a gourmet delicacy served primarily in fancy, upscale restaurants. While having never eaten it myself, I knew that those who had were wealthy and could enjoy very expensive meals. So when the woman told me that her mother desired this delicacy, I assumed two things: she had never tasted pheasant under glass before and she wanted this meal because it was so special.

There are many times in my life when I encounter pheasant–under-glass experiences here on earth. Given to me as special meals of mercy from the Lord of heaven, I relish them as dearly as I did the French cruller that day. Many times, when listening to or reading God's Word, I am moved to tears in appreciation for His love and grace toward me—pheasant under glass. When singing a hymn, my heart explodes with gratitude to my precious Jesus—pheasant under glass. Although rocked with trials and deep concerns, when I sense the awesome grace and mercy of the Lord—pheasant under glass. Although my mind races from stress or time constraints, when I am assured of God's comfort and guidance and experience His peace that surpasses all understanding—pheasant under glass. When God seems far away or when life doesn't make sense, the promises of His Word bring forth joy within—pheasant under glass. And when the Holy Spirit reminds me that my loving heavenly Father will always direct my paths—pheasant under glass.

Although flawless, Jesus became flawed. Although innocent, Jesus became sin for us. Although able to walk away, Jesus selflessly obeyed His Father's will. Although bitter the price, He endured the torments of hell and separation from His Father. And why? So we could receive the Father's embrace and all that He desires for us through all eternity.

Not all of these events are dramatic, nor are they always noticeable to others. Yet my heart is filled with awe at the idea of the Almighty God loving me in such incredible ways. Calling me His child, embracing me with His comfort, and empowering me through His Holy Spirit to live the life to which He has called me, I swallow all those pheasant–under-glass experiences with a deep appreciation of His great love for me. I cannot help but say to Him, "Whom have I in heaven but You? And there is nothing on earth that I desire besides You. My flesh and my heart may fail, but [You are] the strength of my heart and my portion forever" (Psalm 73:25–26).

As I remember the amazing love, hope, and grace that God gives through Scripture, I rejoice in the beautiful passage in Psalm 119:103: "How sweet are Your words to my taste, sweeter than honey to my mouth!" Acknowledging His Word as my greatest pheasant-under-glass treasure, I embrace it daily and meditate on it as often as possible. And during sleepless moments at night, I quote memorized passages, reminding myself of the Lord's goodness in my life.

During these times I am reminded that I am blessed. As God

San

touches my heart through His Word—even when my feelings go against what I know in my heart—I know He is in me and I am in Him. In His Word, He promises He will never leave me nor forsake me; He promises to be my fortress; He assures me that His Holy Spirit has made His light shine in my heart, giving me knowledge of the glory of God in the face of Christ. And He accomplishes this in my jar of clay—frail, cracked, and vulnerable (2 Corinthians 4:6–7). It is that knowledge of Him that opens the windows of heaven and feeds my soul with the richest of fare—even pheasant under glass.

When my heart yearns for a testimony of the living God, I remember an event that happened two thousand years ago when God our Father gave us His very best. Desiring that all His human creatures be redeemed, He sent His Son to be born of a woman, to be born under the Law, and to lie in a manger. In His prayer time, in His experience in the temple, in desert and on mountaintops, the Son listened to His Father and obeyed. Keeping the Law perfectly for us, Jesus continued in His earthly journey, although rejected and ridiculed by those whom He loved, even those who refused to believe in Him. But nothing would stop His journey for humankind's salvation. Nothing would stand in the way of His revealed love for them.

Then, on a hill far away, the Father delivered to the Son not the best but the worst. Knowing and loving that Son from eternity, He allowed—no, required—that Jesus pay the ultimate sacrifice for our sin. Although flawless, Jesus became flawed. Although innocent, Jesus became sin for us. Although able to walk away, Jesus selflessly obeyed His Father's will. Although bitter the price, He endured the torments of hell and the separation from His Father. And why? So we could receive the Father's embrace and receive all that He desires for us through all eternity.

What does this mean for you today? Not only do you receive all those pheasant-under-glass experiences, but you also can dedicate your life in service to Him. Through the study of His Word, taste and see that the Lord is good. Offer your body as a living sacrifice to Him—not out of obligation but out of love for the

San

salvation you have already received. Fix your eyes on Jesus, the author and perfecter of your faith. Assured of God's mercy, grace, and love, you now can love Him and show His love to others. By God's grace you have kissed God's Son—through the undeserved gift of faith. And when your time for heaven comes, pheasant under glass will be just the beginning.

Prayer: Dear Father in heaven, You rejoiced in Your Son's Baptism and transfiguration, and we rejoice that we have been redeemed through His blood. Through Your Holy Spirit, enable us to cherish the hope we receive through the cross and resurrection as we continue to kiss the Son through the faith we have received from You. In His name we pray. *Amen.*

Personal Study Questions:
Psalm 2:12

1. Today's faith narrative suggests that God the Father delivered "the worst" to His Son on Calvary. How does thinking about that make the Gospel account more meaningful for you?

2. The kiss this verse demands from us was considered a sign of submission and is related to the fear of God—an attitude of reverence, awe, and faith.

   a. Where in verse 12 do you find words of Law—God's commands and threats?

   b. Where in this same verse do you read words of Gospel—God's Good News of love and acceptance for Jesus' sake?

3. How do you take refuge in your Messiah-King? In doing that, how have you been blessed?

Group Bible Study for Week 1
Psalm 2

1. As you spent time reading and meditating on Psalm 2 this past week, how did your relationship with your Messiah-King grow in deeper intimacy? How did your understanding of His mission and authority grow?

2. The psalm follows two separate tracks—the divine and the human. We see events on earth and, simultaneously, events in heaven.

    a. Describe events and attitudes on earth, beginning at verse 1 and continuing to the end of the psalm.

    b. Do the same for events and attitudes in heaven.

    c. Where do you see yourself in the psalm?

3. Reread verses 1–6.

    a. Describe the rebellion detailed here.

    b. How do you understand the derision, the scoffing of heaven in verse 4? Why does God laugh?

    c. The Word of God exerts more power than any army, bomb, or other "invincible" weapon human beings can invent. By His Word, God created the Universe (Genesis 1:1–30). By His Word, Jesus controls the weather (Mark 4:35), forgives sins (Mark 2:9–12), and heals diseases (Matthew 8:5–13). By His Word, the Lord will one day dissolve His current creation and establish a home for righteousness (Jeremiah 25:30–38). How does this help to explain the terror noted in Psalm 2:5? Who is terrified?

4. Why does the thought of Christ's ultimate and total rule terrorize people in our world? Where do you see that reflected in the media or in the words and actions of people you know personally?

5. Reread verses 7–12.

a. In what ways does Christ's rule provoke fear in your heart too?

b. In what ways does it call forth peace and joy? What words from the psalm are of special help in this regard?

6. Tell about a time when you ...

a. were able to "rejoice with trembling" in your Messiah-King (v. 11).

b. found blessing by taking "refuge" in Him (v. 12).

Week Two

Psalm 20

[1] May the Lord answer you in the day of trouble!
May the name of the God of Jacob protect you!
[2] May He send you help from the sanctuary
and give you support from Zion!
[3] May He remember all your offerings
and regard with favor your burnt sacrifices! Selah

[4] May He grant you your heart's desire
and fulfill all your plans!
[5] May we shout for joy over your salvation,
and in the name of our God set up our banners!
May the Lord fulfill all your petitions!

[6] Now I know that the Lord saves His anointed;
He will answer him from His holy heaven
with the saving might of His right hand.
[7] Some trust in chariots and some in horses,
but we trust in the name of the Lord our God.
[8] They collapse and fall,
but we rise and stand upright.

[9] O Lord, save the king!
May He answer us when we call.

Suzanne Yelkin

Psalm 20:1

May the Lord answer you in the day of trouble!
May the name of the God of Jacob protect you!

My Offerings

 loved my husband, Bud. I loved our daughter and our three sons and their wives. I loved our new little grandson. I loved my part-time job as teacher aide and art specialist at the Lutheran school our daughter attended. I loved my involvement at our church. I was the choir director, a committee member, and a member of the missionary society. I loved being a student at the nearby Lutheran college. I was working toward a degree that would land me a full-time job with the local Lutheran school system. I loved attending worship services, especially

since I had a hand in the music. I was in love with myself, an exemplary Christian. Life had never been better for me than it was that winter.

The day was exceptionally warm and sunny for a Nebraska February. Bud had gone to town to help our pastor with a small project at the parsonage. When he did not return as soon as expected, I could not contain my impatience. On this rare middle-of-the-week day off from work, we planned to ride. It would be the horses, the trail, and us. When I called the parsonage, he promised to be home soon.

Bud met me at the fence where I had his dapple-gray paint gelding, Chief, and my golden-girl quarter horse, Jackie, tied, saddled, and anxious to go. He was so late that my mood was sour, but seeing that our little cockapoo had decided to join us cheered me. Buster, better known on trail rides as Scout, loved scampering ahead of the horses and circling back to see if we would catch up with him. The trails on our acreage run through brush and trees, up and down mild slopes along a creek, and out into a glorious pasture where we can work up some speed. Bud was ahead of me on Chief. My tension was melting away, and I decided to let loose. I gave Jackie the signal, and she broke into a gallop along the fence line. I concentrated on the posts whipping by, urging her gently with the reins not to get too close. I was not concentrating on my stance and realized too late that my boots had slipped out of the stirrups. I was riding with no control. My mare sped on and I landed hard on my rear end. I briefly lost consciousness after hitting my head when the momentum sent me backward off the horse. I was sitting with my head on my knees when Bud rode up leading Jackie by the reins.

"If you don't get up now and ride her to the pen, you won't want to ride again," he stated, affirming common wisdom.

"Just give me a minute to get my legs back," I snapped as I struggled to my feet.

"You better get back on right now before you talk yourself out of it," he insisted.

By that time, my balance had returned, so I took the reins he offered and mounted the mare, gingerly lowering my sore backside into the saddle. I could see that Bud was not pleased with me for my foolish lapse of judgment. I was not a seasoned enough rider to handle the speed of a sustained full gallop. Because my sour mood had returned, I could not see his concern for me. We rode to the horse stalls in silence. I love the mingled smell of sweet hay and tangy horse sweat, but this time it nauseated me as we brushed the horses down. I soon became aware that I could not see the currycomb in my hand. I also could not see that I was facing the grimmest challenge of my life so far.

Jesus gave me the medicine I needed. He led me, one of His baptized, to His sanctuary, to Zion, to the place where I could receive the gifts He offered.

By March, I quit my job. I had always hated it anyway, I reasoned. After all, I was only one year away from earning my master's degree from a synodical university. Working as a teacher's aide was certainly beneath my ability. In June, I made it to the classes I needed to complete my degree, but I did not follow through with the writings. By fall, when choir was supposed to resume, I backed out, leaving someone else to fill in as director. I quit attending meetings. I backed out of the rest of my life as well. I left my husband without a loving wife, my young daughter without a nurturing mom, my sons and daughters-in-law without the caring ear they were accustomed to, and my grandson without his grandma.

At first, I did not see the downhill slide. Sometime shortly after the accident, a migraine became my constant companion. When our family doctor could not help, I made the rounds of neurologists, psychiatrists, and headache specialists, who offered a cornucopia of the latest pharmaceuticals. Nothing touched the pain. It became so intense and debilitating that I did not want food and could not sleep. I became depressed and anxious. The psychiatrists told us that I had been depressed all my life. Tests showed no damage to my brain. The fall was just the catalyst that intensified the underlying problem. I was self-centered and self-obsessed.

Whatever the truth was, with the headaches came the de-

Suzanne

pression, anger, fear, and hate inside me that the doctors pointed to in order to arrive at a diagnosis. I lashed out at those closest to me. My husband and our daughter were the nearest targets. Bud understood that I was in pain and, true to our wedding vows, stayed with me in this sickness. Our daughter, who was still in elementary school when the accident happened, grew distant as the years passed. By junior high, she did not know how to love the woman her mother had become and she went her own way. She spent most of her time with friends I did not even know.

Sometimes Bud urged me to stay in bed on Sunday mornings because of the pain. In my devastated state, I thought that everyone in church had turned their backs on me as I had on them. It would have been easy to stay away. I hated them and I hated being there, but Jesus would not let me back out of the Divine Service too. Every Sunday, I sat in the pew self-possessed and crying inside. I could not pray except to say, "Look at my sacrifices, God. I have lost my job, my education, and even my daughter. I have lost loving feelings toward her and everyone else. These are my sacrifices and offerings. They are great. Don't you see the things I have done for You? Wasn't I a good and faithful Christian? Why have You allowed everyone to turn away from me? Why have You turned away from me too?"

I did not know that my college community, our daughter's school community, our church, our families, our friends, and Jesus Himself were constantly interceding on my behalf. Jesus gave me the medicine I needed. He led me, one of His baptized, to His sanctuary, to Zion, to the place where I could receive the gifts He offered. Every Sunday, I heard the Good News that even my sinful hate was forgiven through Jesus' death on the cross. I received in my mouth the living body and blood of Jesus Christ, given and shed for the forgiveness of all my sins. I heard the Word that proclaimed the only sacrifice and offering acceptable to God was the death of His only Son, Jesus. The Father heard the prayers of His faithful Son, who said, "I died for this one." Gradually my prayers became, "Father, forgive me for Jesus' sake." He still forgives me. He continually remembers Jesus' offering of His body and blood

Suzanne

on the cross and regards me with favor because of Jesus' sacrifice.

It has been years since my recovery. The horses are gone. Buster is too old and blind now to play scout. A lingering migraine-type eye disturbance is still with me. The headaches are gone. The cause and cure are mysteries to my doctor. Sometimes I feel the weight of depression and the panic of anxiety, but I suppose that is familiar to most people. My faithful husband and I have five more grandchildren. Our oldest will be in middle school this fall. He and his cousins like to spend time with me. We do art projects. We dig snow tunnels in the winter and splash in the horse tank in the summer. Our sons are glad their slightly wacky mother is back. I pray to be a good mother-in-law. Our daughter and I enjoy a love deeper than I thought possible. I said a prayer of thanksgiving as she knelt next to me to receive Holy Communion two Sundays ago. I pray for all of them that God's will be done in their lives. Jesus prays for all of them. He prays for you. Hear God's Word of forgiveness for Jesus' sake. You are protected by the name of the God of Jacob—God the Father, the Son, and the Holy Spirit.

Prayer: Almighty God, keep Your name holy among us, grant us a steadfast faith in Jesus Christ, and protect us from evil, through Jesus Christ our Lord. *Amen.*

Suzanne

Personal Study Questions:
Psalm 20:1

Upon first reading it, this psalm may seem like a message taken from a greeting card we might send to a friend about to undertake a new, challenging task. But as we read more deeply, we come to see the words as they truly are—a prophecy focused on the Messiah. And then, in Him, focused on us as well!

1. "The day of trouble" (v. 1) is any day trouble invades our lives.

   a. What days of trouble does today's faith narrative describe?

   b. What days of trouble did our Lord Jesus experience while He lived here on earth?

2. In what way(s) might you personally consider today a day of trouble?

3. How did the Father answer Jesus in His day of trouble? When He answers you today, what do you hope He will do for you?

4. The Messiah's name is Jesus (Savior). How does that name protect you?

Suzanne

Psalm 20:2–5

*May He send you help from the sanctuary and give
you support from Zion! May He grant you your heart's
desire and fulfill all your plans! May we shout for joy
over your salvation, and in the name of our God set up
our banners! May the LORD fulfill all your petitions!*

My Heart's Desire

Like everyone else, I have desires and plans. Some of those desires are charitable, and my plans often involve being good to someone else. However, sinner that I am, my plans and desires are always tainted with selfishness. The older I get, my heart's desire is to be able to find everything I misplace. It is the usual—car keys, my watch, a book, or the check for winning the local poetry contest. (That one is really nagging me.)

About a year ago, I thought I had lost my purse for good. I came home from work at the after-school day-

Suzanne

54

care. Three of my favorite guys, my husband and two of our sons, were on the top of our two-story house, where they were finishing putting on a new roof. They were hot and tired and wanted a cold beverage so they could relax and admire their work. Since I was on the ground, I was chosen to get it. I grabbed three cold ones from the fridge and started up the ladder. I did not take note of where I set my purse because I was concentrating on getting those drinks up the ladder. I am afraid of heights. Halfway up, my knees started to knock. "O God," I prayed, "please don't let me fall," and right then I stopped at the top of the first story. One of my sons had to come halfway down. I was traumatized by the height, and by the time my feet touched the blessed ground, I had completely forgotten about my purse. "Thank You, God!" I breathed.

The next day as I prepared to go to work, I could not locate my purse anywhere. Time was running short. "God, forgive me," I prayed, and I drove to the daycare without my license. The next day went pretty much the same with no purse and no license. I called my cell phone, which was in my purse, hoping to hear it ring. "Help me find it, Lord," I pleaded. When I punched in the numbers, I could hear the faint distinct melody in the distance. I followed the sound to our garage and the shed just beyond it. I searched the car, the truck, and the tractor. There was no purse anywhere. I was still praying about my purse on the way home the third day, "I have so much to lose. Please! Please, let me remember where I left it." Right then it dawned on me. My ringtone was coming from the neighbor's property. Their dog, Horse, so named for his appetite, was a notorious shoe thief. What would stop him from stealing a purse off my porch?

When I arrived home, I crawled through the three-tree-deep windbreak and burst into the neighbor's yard, perspiring and dirty, pine needles in my hair, house phone to my ear, and the sound of my cellular playing in the distance. Upon seeing me, disheveled and gripping the phone, Dave rushed to me from their garage and cried out, "Suzanne, are you all right?"

Well, I can only imagine what he was thinking, but I am sure

Suzanne

by the look on his face that he did not expect me to say, "I'm fine, Dave, I'm just looking for my purse." I quickly told him the story of my search and my suspicions.

Dave knows his dog's faults and was not offended by my accusation. We walked around the house and located the purse. It was under their deck on the back of the house right outside the sliding glass basement doors they seldom use. My purse was completely zipped and everything was in it. Dave shook his head and apologized, adding, "Horse is probably proud of himself. Until now he hasn't taken anything but shoes."

My plans will come up short like a half pair of flip-flops, but God's plan is complete. All believers and I will be with Him, where we belong, just like a matched pair of boots.

I am not proud of my near obsession with lost things. However, sometimes my desire to find what I have misplaced reminds me that God seeks the lost people of this world because He desires that they all be saved. Saint Paul, whose heart's desire was formed by God, prayed for his fellow Jews, "Brothers, my heart's desire and prayer to God for them is that they may be saved. For I bear them witness that they have a zeal for God, but not according to knowledge. For, being ignorant of the righteousness of God, and seeking to establish their own, they did not submit to God's righteousness. For Christ is the end of the law for righteousness to everyone who believes" (Romans 10:1–4).

I know that because of sin I am not righteous. My feeble attempts to establish my own righteousness fail as surely as many of my attempts to find all my lost stuff. No, my righteousness has to come from Jesus, who is truly righteous. The Bible says, "For our sake He made Him to be sin who knew no sin, so that in Him we might become the righteousness of God" (2 Corinthians 5:21). Our righteousness is complete; Jesus is the end, the fulfillment of the Law. I shout for joy that His plans are fulfilled, I am saved by Jesus' sacrifice for me.

Dave came around again the other day with a box of shoes in the back of his pickup truck. Like most of us, he tries to do the right thing. "Do any of these shoes belong to you?" he asked.

Suzanne

I rummaged through the box and found a half-chewed flip-flop that matched one I had thrown away the week before and a boot missing since last winter. "I'll take these," I said, thinking there was no reason to tell him that I would never wear the flip-flop. "Horse is still at it, I see."

"Oh, you mean Thief?" he corrected me.

"That's an appropriate name change," I said as I waved him on his way with a smile.

Jesus' banner of righteousness waves over me. In Him, my name is changed from Sinner to Saint. Although I will continue to sin as surely as Thief will continue to steal shoes, God forgives me. I know because I will hear the blessed words of Absolution for Jesus' sake from my pastor again this week. My plans will come up short like a half pair of flip-flops, but God's plan is complete. All believers and I will be with Him, where we belong, just like a matched pair of boots.

I will continue to pray, "Thy will be done," because in Christ, I am a righteous saint. Thanks be to God! By the way, I found my fifteen-dollar check today. I am still praying about what to do with it. Truly, out of grace God does grant our hearts' desires and in His wisdom fulfils His plans for us.

Prayer: O Lord, I shout for joy in Your salvation. Create in me a clean heart and a right spirit so my desires are formed by Your Word. You called me in my Baptism to be Your own. You feed me with the holy life-giving body and blood of Your Son, Jesus. Hold Your banner over me all the days of my life, and grant that Your gifts sustain me in the faith unto life everlasting. Bless Your Word wherever it is proclaimed, so hearts receive Jesus Christ in faith. In His name. **Amen.**

Suzanne

tuesday

Personal Study Questions:
Psalm 20:2–5

1. The Lord sent angels from heaven's sanctuary to serve Jesus (Mark 1:13) and to strengthen Him (Luke 22:41–43) in times of trouble and temptation. When have you received hope and help from "Zion"—either directly through the Holy Scriptures or indirectly as a member of Christ's Church encouraged and supported you?

2. Considering that this psalm is Messianic, speaking about Jesus as the promised Savior sent by God the Father, what "offering" or "sacrifice" (verse 3) do we especially want the Father to remember? (Hebrews 9:11-12). How does that offering encourage you when you need "help" and "support" (verse 2)?

3. As you think deeply about the Lord's love for you, do you think you can "shout for joy" (v. 5) over the salvation He has provided? How else will you worship Him?

Psalm 20:6

Now I know that the LORD saves His anointed;
He will answer him from His holy heaven
with the saving might of His right hand.

My Anointing

It surprised me when I realized how much I relied on my own reputation as a responsible citizen. What a shock I received in jail when I realized that I was just another number! I was no different from my cellmate, who was incarcerated on drug charges. It certainly did not matter to the attendants who I was or what I had done. I could have been a murderer.

It all began one cold January morning when my daughter was running late for school. She missed the bus that stops at our driveway, so I planned to drive her to school 12 miles away. By the time I dressed, I knew

we would barely make it on time. When we got into the car, I was careful to set my cruise control on the precise miles-per-hour speed limit so I would not be tempted to drive too fast. I had planned to slow down for the two-block-long rural community we pass through on the way to the junior high. There the speed limit is 35. When we arrived at this community, I dutifully hit the brakes and slowed down to the posted speed. I do not know what I was thinking after that, but as I revved up to highway speed again, I unfortunately forgot about cruise control. When I was stopped, the polite young officer gave me a ticket for going 75 in a 55-mile-an-hour speed zone. He said he was feeling generous because I was going closer to 80! I think he knew that I was not a habitual speeder.

He told me I could pay the $120 fine through the mail as soon as I received notice that the ticket was on file with the county court. Otherwise, I would be required to appear before the judge in person to contest the ticket. The court date listed was a Wednesday in February at nine in the morning. In the meantime, while I waited for confirmation of the filing, I talked to a friend who worked at the courthouse. She told me that I could save the money by sitting two hours in jail. Well, I did not intend to do that!

The morning of the court date, I called the county offices because I had never received confirmation by mail. Sure enough, no one knew why, but the ticket had not been filed. I would have to appear in person. In my naiveté, I thought I would be the only one there for the nine-o'clock appointment. I was surprised to see the courtroom filled with traffic offenders facing charges of drunk driving, reckless driving, driving on suspended license, and worse. Everyone seemed to have an attorney except me. The court's docket was full, and the hours ticked away. Most of the cases were held over for trial because many defendants pleaded not guilty to their charges. I think I may have snoozed a bit because around eleven-thirty I was jolted awake by the sound of someone calling my name. I looked around and saw that I was the next to last person still seated. I cautiously walked forward.

I do not remember the swearing in, but I am sure that I said I would tell the truth.

After reading the particulars of my case, the judge, looking slightly bored and hungry, asked me, "How do you plead?"

I said, "I did it, so I am guilty."

This perked her up, and she asked with a puzzled look, "Why did you come to court then?"

I replied, "I had to because the ticket was never filed with the court."

Immediately she called for a recess to investigate the matter.

"Court will resume in fifteen minutes," she said.

Fifteen minutes later, I was back on the stand.

"I apologize to you," the judge said. "You are right. I don't know why, but your ticket was never filed. It should have been. I am sorry you had to make the trip and spend the morning in my courtroom, but I have to impose a fine of $120 anyway."

"Okay," I said, not quite understanding the suppressed laughter around me. I think I made that judge's day.

"You can pay your fine at the clerk's office or sit out the ticket," she said.

"She never apologizes," a lawyer whispered to me in awe as I left the room.

Well, that is one point for me, I thought, feeling pretty special.

I was looking for the clerk's office when a thought hit me. *I could earn sixty dollars an hour if I sat this out.* I had never earned that much per hour in my life, and the thought made me feel even more special. Besides, my friend's words came back to me, "They won't have time to book you in if they are busy. They will take your name and let you sit in the waiting room two hours for a speeding ticket. Register at four o'clock, and you will be out by six." The courthouse looked busy that day, so I thought, *Why not?* After lunch and a couple errands, I would head for the jail.

I was dressed for church that evening: nice skirt, lacy blouse, a vest, my coat, and fashion boots. Feeling confident, I walked to the jail waiting room desk, my ticket in hand. There were several people already seated. I was sure I would join them. The clerk took

Suzanne

my ticket and motioned for me to sit down. Ten minutes later, she called my name. I thought she was going to have me sign something, but she escorted me through a door that led to the cells. I stood in front of a high counter and felt small.

"Remove the coat, vest, boots, jewelry, watch, and stockings," the officer said. I looked up at her in disbelief and read the name on her badge.

This experience caused to me to appreciate even more that my name is Christian. My identity is forever written in God's book of life. He knows my fingerprints and my face. He even knows how many hairs are on my head.

"But, Officer Rita," I stammered, realizing too late that it was the wrong thing to say.

"Hand over the purse and gloves too," she snapped, indicating a basket for my things.

She led me away. I felt ashamed, naked, and nameless.

I will not repeat the language my cellmate used. She was a nice girl, she said. Her no-good boyfriend set her up for the drug deal.

"I'm a seamstress. I've got a wedding to sew for in a month and I'm looking at ten to twenty," she spat out bitterly. "What are you in for?"

"Uh, speeding. One hundred in a thirty-five," I lied, feeling that I needed a reputation.

She shook her head in disbelief at such stupidity. "They'll be bringing dinner. Don't eat the stuff they call chicken. Bread's not bad though—homemade."

The bread was good, but I ate the dinner with little enthusiasm. I was starting to feel abandoned. Right after dinner, they came to get me. I thought it was time to go. Instead, they sat me down for a mug shot and pressed my fingers onto an inkpad. I now have a mug shot, a number, and my fingerprints on file.

Next, they led me to a holding cell the size of a phone booth.

"I'll be back in twenty minutes to process your release," Officer Rita told me.

I nodded back.

The minutes ticked by as long as hours. No one came.

Gloom engulfed me and I prayed, "God, they have forgotten me. Please don't forsake me too."

Suzanne

Just when hope waned, Officer Rita unlocked my cell door and escorted me to freedom.

"Thank You, God, they remembered my name and set me free," I prayed silently.

This experience caused to me to appreciate even more that my name is Christian. My identity is forever written in God's book of life. He knows my fingerprints and my face. He even knows how many hairs are on my head.

Jesus, the Anointed One, was forsaken on the cross for my sake. He rose again so I, too, may live. God saved His Son, King Jesus, and He saves me. No matter where I find myself, even in a jail cell for my careless mistakes, I know that the Holy Spirit anointed me with faith in my Baptism. Jesus stands before the throne of God in heaven to plead my case. God's verdict is "not guilty."

That evening, at the chancel rail in my church sanctuary for the Ash Wednesday service, I still felt small, a naked sinner at the throne of God.

Pastor spoke, "From dust you came and to dust you shall return," as he smeared ashes into the sign of the cross on my forehead. Yes, I am dust, but this dust will live unto eternity because in Christ, God's right hand is mighty to save.

Prayer: Almighty God and Father, You have called me by name in my Baptism. I am guilty of the most heinous sins of thought, word, and deed. I deserve the consequences of my sin here on earth and for eternity. Free me and all people locked in the prison of their sins with the unlocking key of Your forgiveness. In the name of Jesus and for His sake. Amen.

Suzanne

wednesday

Personal Study Questions:
Psalm 20:6

1. This verse makes it clear the Holy Spirit intends that the entire psalm refer to the Messiah, His "Anointed One." How was Jesus' resurrection proof positive that the Lord "saves His anointed" and will also save you? (See 1 Peter 1:20–21.)

2. When have you realized both your guilt and the freedom of release in a way similar to that described in today's faith narrative?

3. Jesus prays for you constantly (Hebrews 7:24–25). God answers His Son's prayers (Psalm 20:6). How do these twin truths hearten you and give you hope today?

Psalm 20:7–8

Some trust in chariots and some in horses,
but we trust in the name of the LORD our God.
They collapse and fall, but we rise and stand upright.

My Trust

I had just gotten off the phone with my oldest sister. Once again, my eyes burned, and I had a hard time swallowing. She lives half the country away in an institution on the West Coast. I rarely have the means to fly out to see her, so I call her every week.

Those of us who deal with a family member's or their own mental illness understand that life is in God's hands. No portion of life is really in our control, not even the smallest detail.

Lynn is eight years older than I am. Of course, when I was little, I looked up to her. Who wouldn't idolize their big sister, especially if she was a beautiful and pop-

ular high school cheerleader and a sweetheart dance queen? Lynn had always wanted to be a reporter, so her decision to become a nurse surprised us. When she was in nurses' training, occasionally Lynn would let me stay with her in her dorm over the weekend. I was the darling of the floor, and I loved all the attention from the other girls. Her classmates loved her for her lively spirit and kindness. Lynn had her share of dates, and she eventually went steady with a nice young man from our hometown. He sometimes gave me a ride home after these visits. I looked forward to Lynn's graduation and marriage to him. I trusted that they would live in a town only 30 miles away from us where he was a reporter and editor for a small newspaper. To everyone's surprise, though, she chose to marry a premed student. We did not know him very well, but we trusted that she had made a good choice.

After their first son was born, Lynn and her family moved to the East Coast so her husband could pursue his career at an Ivy League university. Shortly after the birth of their second son, we began to receive telephone calls from her that troubled us greatly. At first, because she was so far away from home, none of us recognized these calls as early signs of mental illness.

When she said on the phone, "A movie director followed me home from work tonight. He wants me to be an actress," we thought it was strange but, somehow, possible.

Denial caused us to ignore the more bizarre calls.

"A man living in the building across the street reads my thoughts," she claimed. Statements such as, "I am being followed by the FBI because I know government secrets," were intertwined with news of her children, husband, and work.

The events of the next few years are hard to piece together. After her husband received his doctorate, they moved back to our home state. He was a resident doctor at the state university hospital. We trusted that their lives would be filled with success and happiness.

By then, I was married and had young children. On visits to her house, she would lead us on a scavenger hunt or out to fly a kite. The only way I can describe her beautiful house is to say that

Suzanne

it always appeared as if they had just moved in. Meals there were sporadic. While I noticed these things, I did not want to criticize. She continued to work as a nurse but frequently changed jobs. We failed to see her impetuosity and unstable nature as warning signs of an even greater problem. Even when her behavior became too bizarre to ignore, our family did not talk about it. The stigma of her potential illness was too great. I think we trusted that her husband would handle it and that she would be all right. However, eventually her husband divorced her, and she lost custody of her two sons.

It is hard to put twenty years of tumult into words. Shortly after the divorce, Lynn left for Hollywood, deluded into thinking she could be a movie star. We didn't hear from her for weeks at a time. My parents spent many anxious days looking for her in the city. They found her, brought her home, and sought help for her. They put her in the care of a doctor they trusted at a good psychiatric hospital. However, the hospital could not legally keep her against her will. This cycle played out many times. She always returned to her dream.

Now, Lynn is physically disabled and confined to a wheelchair. She likes the sunny weather of Los Angeles and seems happy when I call. Our dad died years ago, and our mom is in her nineties. Mom takes comfort in the fact that Lynn cannot return to life in the streets. More important, she has always taken comfort in the fact of Lynn's Baptism. I confess that I was not always so comforted. Over the years, I often engaged in "if only" thinking. If only Lynn had pursued a career in journalism and married the nice boyfriend from our hometown. If only her husband had been as understanding as mine, who stayed by me during terrible illness. If only he had gotten help for her instead of divorcing her. If only our parents had stepped in after the first warning signs. If only our whole family had talked openly about her behavior. If only the laws had been on our side. If only I had been a better sister and insisted on care for her sooner. If only I had listened more closely when Lynn talked to me. If only the new psychiatric drugs had existed when she needed help. If only she had stayed in our

Suzanne

67

home state. *If only.*

Now, when I call Lynn on the telephone, we talk mostly of childhood memories, good coffee, and faith. During our last call, she apologized for her part in locking me in the basement bathroom of our hometown's aging theater. I was five. To this day, I can still see the glare of the bare lightbulb hanging overhead and the extra theater seats stacked and dusty behind a heavy curtain.

When we were infants, our parents, trusting God's Word, brought us to the font where we were baptized in His name. We belong to Jesus. He loves my sisters. He loves me. . . . Here we stand, firmly, by His grace.

"I'm sorry it scared you so much," she says. "You were only in there a minute."

"It was ten minutes at least!" I protest, laughing. Lynn laughs too.

"Do you remember when I made you that cheerleading outfit? I wanted you to be our mascot, but you were too shy to do the cheers in front of the crowd," she reminds me. "You have always been a little scaredy-cat."

"I have not!" I deny.

Yes, Lynn, I have been afraid, I think. *There were times I was afraid you were gone forever.*

"Did they bring your morning coffee yet?" I ask, sipping mine.

"They just brought it," she replies, "There is nothing better than a good cup of coffee."

"That's for sure; we can share a cup over the phone." I agree. "What have you been reading lately?"

"They have some magazines here. There was an article on the shortage of nurses. I think I will look into getting my license again and go back to work," she says, unaware that this will certainly never happen.

"There is a Bible here too, but I would like one of my own again," she adds.

"I'll send you one," I say, making a mental note to do that for her.

"I like to go to the chapel services here; we sing hymns that I know, like 'Jesus Loves Me' and 'I am Jesus Little Lamb.' Jesus

Suzanne

loves me, Suzie," she proclaims.

"Yes, He does, Lynn," I choke out the words.

Mom has been right all along. Even through the heart-break, she has always known where to put her trust concerning her children. When we were infants, our parents, trusting God's Word, brought us to the font where we were baptized in His name. We belong to Jesus. He loves my sisters. He loves me. What the psalmist says is true. Those who trust in chariots and horses will fall, and those who trust in the name of the Lord our God will stand upright. Here we stand, firmly, by His grace.

Prayer: Almighty and merciful God, through Baptism You put Your name on us and promise to be with us. Comfort your children who are afflicted by mental illness. Help them and all of us, your servants, to stand firm in our Baptism, our shield against the taunts of the devil. Direct our trust to You alone. Through Jesus Christ, our Lord. *Amen.*

Suzanne

thursday

Personal Study Questions:
Psalm 20:7–8

1. Twice in this psalm (vv. 1 and 7), the writer mentions the "name" of the Lord providing refuge and protection. Why is the name important and powerful?

2. When did God place that name upon you?

3. How does it comfort you to know you bear that name?

Psalm 20:9

O Lord, save the king!
May He answer us when we call.

My King!

L ate one summer, my husband, Bud, took up bird-watching. A friend's display of finches inspired him to get bags of thistle and sunflower seeds, a birdbath, and four feeders. Bud hung the feeders from the crossbars of my clothesline and hoped for goldfinches and cardinals. A week passed with no customers. Then one morning, I spotted a male goldfinch. He sampled the treats cau-

Suzanne

71

tiously, then voraciously. His lovely bride joined him next. A couple of days later, we heard a commotion in the pines. Several finches were having a twitter fit, no doubt discussing the merits of eating from our feeders. Come and eat, the first bird must have told them. There is plenty for all! Drink the water! It is good and fresh!

Bud became so engrossed with his hobby that he dubbed himself a "finch man." That was when my competitive nature was aroused. That year, our oldest son had given me a hummingbird feeder for Mother's Day and I decided to get in on the game. I mixed the correct portions of water and sugar and boiled it exactly two minutes. I filled the feeder bulb, screwed on the feeding stations, and hung the hummingbird feeder from a bracket on a porch post. My hummingbirds came that day. Ironically, my hummingbirds like Bud better than me. They buzz up to him while he is enjoying his morning coffee on the porch. They are not shy in the least.

Once, when I was about ten, I saved a hummingbird's life. My mom will vouch that I am telling the truth. She discovered it beating its wings against the garage ceiling. We tried shooing it out the open door but it would not fly away. So, we came up with a rescue plan. I cut a hole in the bottom of a shoebox. Teetering on a stepladder that Mom held steady, I trapped the bird in the box against the ceiling. I reached in to grab it. Both the bird and I trembled as my hand wrapped around its body.

I did not dare to breathe as I stepped out into the sunlight. For a brief moment, the hummingbird sat still in my open hand. Its perfect wings shimmered iridescent. Then, like a tiny helicopter, the hummingbird shot straight up and looked me in the eye. It beeped at me, either to thank or scold.

"It was so beautiful, Mom. Did you see its wings?" I finally let go of my breath as I asked.

"It is one of God's most loveliest creatures," she agreed. "You were very gentle; it wasn't hurt at all."

"Did you hear it squeak at me?"

"It said thanks," she said, smiling.

"I think it did too." I agreed, laughing.

Suzanne

72

Now I have turned into the all-time hummingbird champion. Just yesterday, my cat crouched to spring at a ruby-throat hovering around the feeder. I ran for the spray bottle and squirted water on Kitty right between the eyes. Sputtering, she lost her balance and fell off the porch. True to her nature as a cat, Kitty landed on all fours and tried to slink away. I looked up to see how the bird fared, just in time to watch it dive-bomb the poor cat. I thought. This incident reminded me of my earlier hummingbird rescue. Mom will be glad that I haven't forgotten how it felt to save a hummingbird's life. I felt awestruck.

Even more awesome is that the Lord God Almighty holds us in His hand. At Matins every Tuesday morning, our small group, led by our pastor, sings the Venite: "The Lord is a great God, and a great king above all gods. The deep places of the earth are in His hand; the strength of the hills is His also. The sea is His, for He made it, and His hand formed the dry land. For He is our God, and we are the people of His pasture and the sheep of His hand" (based on Psalm 95:1–7).

Gently, the Lord opens His hand and lets us go into the world to live out our lives. We daily go our own sinful way. Like the hummingbird that dive-bombed the cat, we like to think we are self-reliant. We will never know how many times He has saved us from earthly peril, yet we know we need God's protection and forgiveness. His holy angels watch over us, and He Himself is always with us. Jesus, our once dead and now risen Savior-King, said, "Behold, I am with you always, to the end of the age" (Matthew 28:20). The Father saved His Son, our King. Jesus is with us to answer us when we call.

Other birds have come to our yard since our bird-watching adventure began. This week we have a large congregation of finches and cardinals at the feeders and birdbath. The shy cardinals show up in pairs. During one afternoon of bird-watching, Bud witnessed a scarlet male that pulled seeds from the feeder and flew back and forth to the female, which was camouflaged in a nearby tree. At first, it looked to Bud as if the male kissed the female each time. Then he realized the male was carrying food to her.

Suzanne

73

"I think he is protecting her as well as feeding her," Bud said.

"That makes sense," I replied.

Jesus protects His Church, His Bride. Through her, He invites the world to come and listen to God's Word. He feeds us as we gather there. We confess the true words of Jesus that instituted the Sacrament of the Lord's Supper. Through my pastor last Sunday, I heard Jesus say, "Take and eat, this is My body given for you. Take and drink, this is My blood shed for the forgiveness of your sins."

When I go my own way, when I think I can take care of myself, when my sinful nature leads me away from Jesus, my protector, the Groom and the Bride say, "Come and eat, come and drink. There is enough for all! This is for the forgiveness of all your sins."

Although I was not enthusiastic at first, I am glad Bud has taken up this new hobby. I haven't used my clothesline since the feeders went up, but our birds have caused me to ponder God's love, protection, and salvation through Jesus Christ, our King. I am reminded to thank Him for all He has done.

"Come, let us worship and bow down, let us kneel before the Lord, our maker. For He is our God, and we are the people of His pasture and the sheep of His hand. Glory be to the Father and to the Son and to the Holy Spirit; as it was in the beginning, is now, and will be forever. Amen" (The Venite).

We will never know how many times He has saved us from earthly peril, yet we know we need God's protection and forgiveness. His holy angels watch over us, and He Himself is always with us. Jesus, our once dead and now risen Savior-King, said, "Behold, I am with you always, to the end of the age" (Matthew 28:20).

Prayer: Almighty and everlasting God, You have promised to be with Your people through all the ages. Protect Your Church with Your mighty hand. Keep us steadfast in Your Word. Feed us with Your open hand, and lead us to heaven, where we will celebrate the feast everlasting with Jesus, our King. In His name. **Amen.**

Suzanne

Friday

Personal Study Questions:
Psalm 20:9

1. Because the Lord saved King Jesus, raising **Him from death** (v. 9), we can also trust Him to answer **us when we call**. What will you call on Him to do for **you today in Jesus'** name?

2. How did today's faith narrative help **you more deeply trea-sure** His care for you?

Suzanne

Group Bible Study for Week 2
Psalm 20

1. Psalm 20 begins as a blessing we might speak over our children, a dear friend, or a loved one.

   a. Why would you treasure this blessing or words of benediction (vv. 1–5) being spoken over you?

   b. None of us deserves the gifts from God offered here. Our sins draw down God's curse rather than His blessing. Only Jesus, who lived on our planet as true God, yet at the same time as a true human being, deserved these blessings. Give examples of each blessing coming into Jesus' earthly life. (Skim Matthew, Mark, Luke, or John if you need help.)

   c. Reread verses 1–5 as though the Holy Spirit were speaking this blessing over Jesus, the Messiah. How does it encourage you to know that from all eternity, the Holy Trinity—Father, Son, and Holy Spirit—has yearned for your salvation, your rescue?

2. Why might the words of Psalm 20:6–9 have been among the words of praise Jesus prayed as He left His tomb on the first Easter morning?

3. Because of the Messiah's "offerings" and "sacrifices" (v. 3) on your behalf, and the "saving might" (v. 6) of the Lord's right hand, this psalm's blessings now belong to you and to all believers in Christ. In His cross, your sins are gone. The curse of sin is removed. The riches of heaven belong to you as your inheritance. Which blessings mentioned in this psalm bring you the most joy? Explain.

4. The "burnt sacrifices" (v. 3) required under the Old Testament ceremonial law represented total devotion to the Lord. The animal was burned completely until neither hide nor hair (literally!) was left!

a. How did Christ Jesus give Himself totally to the Lord?

b. How does the apostle Paul apply this picture directly to us, the redeemed, in Romans 12:1–2?

5. We do not earn salvation through the gifts we give, the offerings we bring, or the deeds of love and kindness we do. Nonetheless, our Lord graciously remembers them, and even rewards us for them! (See Acts 10:4.)

a. God does not need our money or our good works. Even so, He chooses to "regard them with favor"! How does this favor bless you and those around you?

b. Some have thought the term *Selah* means something like "pause and think about this." A musical interlude for thought may have come at this point. If that is indeed true, why do you think the Holy Spirit may have chosen to inspire such an interlude after verse 3?

6. How does this psalm deepen your understanding of and thankfulness for Jesus' love for you? How does it help you see in an even more meaningful way all He has done for you?

Week Three

Psalm 21

[1] O Lord, in Your strength the king rejoices,
and in Your salvation how greatly he exults!
[2] You have given him his heart's desire
 and have not withheld the request of his lips. *Selah*
[3] For You meet him with rich blessings;
You set a crown of fine gold upon his head.
[4] He asked life of You; You gave it to him,
length of days forever and ever.
[5] His glory is great through Your salvation;
splendor and majesty You bestow on him.
[6] For You make him most blessed forever;
You make him glad with the joy of Your presence.
[7] For the king trusts in the Lord,
and through the steadfast love of the Most High he
shall not be moved.

[8] Your hand will find out all Your enemies;
Your right hand will find out those who hate You.
[9] You will make them as a blazing oven
when You appear.
The Lord will swallow them up in His wrath,
and fire will consume them.
[10] You will destroy their descendants from the earth,
and their offspring from among the children of man.
[11] Though they plan evil against You,
though they devise mischief, they will not succeed.
[12] For You will put them to flight;
You will aim at their faces with Your bows.

[13] Be exalted, O Lord, in Your strength!
We will sing and praise Your power.

Adriane Dorr

Psalm 21:1

*O LORD, in Your strength the king rejoices, and
in Your salvation how greatly he exults!*

Dad Can Do It!

If I heard it once as a child, I heard it fifty times: "If you ever need anything, just call Dad." My big, brawny, broad-shouldered father—a 6-foot-2-inch formidable Iowa farmer—was the answer to practically all of my early childhood problems. Bicycle tire gone flat? Dad could fix it. Slimy worm too nasty to put on a hook? Dad could bait it. Older sisters picking on me again? Dad could stop them. There wasn't anything he couldn't do.

I found this to be true even as I grew older and entered high school. Lacking motivation to do homework? Dad had no problem remedying that. Mouthing off to Mom? Dad would definitely take care of that too. And when it came to college visits and talk of financial aid and course schedules, there were few questions Dad couldn't answer in that area either. When I couldn't decide if I should major in law or history, he could see the pros and cons of each. And when I finally narrowed my college choices to two, he made sure no obstacle stood in my way when it came to the final decision.

Leaving for college did not change my view of my father either. Money problems? Professor trouble? Roommate issues? Just call Dad. The little phrase even began to be a part of the saying-good-bye-and-heading-back-to-college ritual that would take place after spring break or Christmas. It usually involved Dad standing at the front door, holding me tightly in a hug, and saying quietly, "Now, just remember: if you ever need anything, who do you call?" And my response was always, "Just call Dad." It was comforting, knowing that he meant it. And I knew that he did. He'd been taking care of things for me since I was born, and there was no reason to believe it would change. He was my dad. There was nothing he couldn't do.

Now that I'm finished with college and living on my own, my dad is still the first person I call when a situation arises. When the grim-faced mechanic said I needed four new tires, only one month after getting three others, I called Dad. When I didn't understand the wording of my insurance policy, I called Dad. When I couldn't get my taxes to make sense, you guessed it. I called Dad. Time and time again, I am convinced that there is nothing he can't do.

Still convinced that there is nothing he can't do, I'm also beginning to realize that my father doesn't reserve this special attention just for me. It's not as though he answers only *my* money questions or fixes *my* school problems or repairs *my* flat tires. He does it for my mom, too, and for my sisters and their husbands,

Adriane

for his grandchildren, and even for his friends. He doesn't greed-ily keep under wraps his understanding of how the world works or his ability to lift and pull and fix practically anything. He uses it to help those around him, if for no other reason than because it gives him joy to do so. He's not stingy when it comes to giving help. In fact, it's quite the opposite—he gives it freely. He doesn't ask for anything in return. A simple thank-you is more than enough.

When the time came for Jesus to journey to the cross, rejected by His friends, His followers, and by His own Father, Jesus was strong. When He hung on the cross—weak, wet with blood, and wavering between life and death—He was strong. And now that He has risen from the dead, proclaiming defeat of that frightening trinity of the devil, the world, and our sinful nature, He is strong.

So it is with a bit of somberness that I reflect on the fact that one day my tough, strong father will re-alize that he's grown old and is no longer able to fix tractors or build bookcases or unload trailers full of his daughter's mostly useless items. But I take joy in know-ing that he'll still be strong in the ways that matter be-yond this life. He'll hold fast to his belief that Baptism saves, that the true God is triune—Father, Son, and Holy Spirit—and that Jesus forgives his sins through the Lord's Supper. He'll remind me that I ought to be doing my devotions. He'll reiterate the importance of maintaining our family's religious heritage. He'll repeat the value of singing hymns while gathered around the piano. And he won't shy away from telling me that one day we'll all be together in the mansion our heavenly Father has prepared for us.

You may have had similar experiences with your own fathers or uncles or brothers. Yet while each of us probably looks up to and admires our fathers or father figures for all their strength, remembering as little girls that awe of their ability to fix practically anything, it is far more comforting to know that we have a heavenly Father whose strength will never fade and who can fix anything, even our sin.

So why do we so often find it easier to question our Lord's strength than that of our human fathers? If God knew how hard your aunt's death would be for you, why did He let her die? If He's truly God, why doesn't He make your fiancé stop arguing with

Adriane

you? And if He's really strong enough to part the Red Sea, why can't He get your mother to stop criticizing how you make mashed potatoes?

Stop. Repent. Remember what He has done for you. When you couldn't withstand the temptation to covet your best friend's new designer purse, He forgave you. When you were supposed to take care of your client's file and forgot, blaming it on your co-worker instead, He forgave you. When your son carelessly spilled lemonade on your newly mopped kitchen floor and you snapped at him in anger, He forgave you. All of these things—these sinful actions that required more strength to withstand than you possess—He has taken care of on your behalf.

But it doesn't end there. When the time came for Jesus to journey to the cross, rejected by His friends, His followers, and by His own Father, Jesus was strong. When He hung on the cross—weak, wet with blood, and wavering between life and death—He was strong. And now that He has risen from the dead, proclaiming defeat of that frightening trinity of the devil, the world, and our sinful nature, He is strong. Jesus is strong like His Father is strong—strong for you.

So maybe terrorists will wage war against us or neighbors speak lies about us. Bosses may fire us. Sisters may pit themselves against us. Children may yell at us. Drivers may cut in front of us. Friends may judge us. Politicians may deceive us. Salesmen may cheat us. Yet through all of this, we rest in the security of our Lord and His strength, knowing that when we need anything, we can call on Him. Remember the words of Mary in Luke 1:49–53:

> *"For He who is mighty has done great things for me, and holy is His name. And His mercy is for those who fear Him from generation to generation. He has shown strength with His arm; He has scattered the proud in the thoughts of their hearts; He has brought down the mighty from their thrones and exalted those of humble estate; He has filled the hungry with good things, and the rich He has sent away empty."*

Adriane

We have a Father who is stronger than even the burliest of dads. His strong love for us sent His Son to the cross. Bookcases, taxes, and U-Haul fix-its may be the work of our earthly fathers, but forgiveness, life, and salvation are the work of our heavenly Father. There's truly nothing He can't do!

Prayer: Heavenly Father, in my human weakness, I can't comprehend the scope of Your strength. You are strong enough to part seas and move mountains. You are strong enough to hold the heavens in balance. And You are strong enough to send Your only Son to the cross to bear the weight and pain of all the world's sin. Thank You, Lord, for the forgiveness and mercy and promise of salvation that are mine through Jesus. In His name I pray. Amen.

Adriane

Personal Study Questions:
Psalm 21:1

1. How does the author of today's faith narrative identify with Psalm 21? What connections does she see with her own life?

2. Think about the challenges you face right now. For which of these could you take comfort and find strength from the faith narrative and psalm verse?

3. We might consider this messianic psalm a post-resurrection or even post-ascension hymn of praise to our Savior and about our Savior.

   a. How do the first two verses hint at this?

   b. See 1 Timothy 2:3–4. What was (and is!) Christ's "heart's desire" (Psalm 21:2)?

Adriane

Psalm 21:2–5

You have given him his heart's desire and have not withheld the request of his lips. For You meet him with rich blessings; You set a crown of fine gold upon his head. He asked life of You; You gave it to him, length of days forever and ever. His glory is great through Your salvation; splendor and majesty You bestow on him.

But I Want It!

It's practically impossible to say no to a baby. Consider, for instance, my nephew, Oliver. He's eight-months old with nearly white hair and robin's egg blue eyes and a two-tiny-toothed smile that could melt icebergs in the Antarctic. People very rarely refuse him a thing simply because he's so stinking cute. In restaurants, waitresses stop to tickle him. In department stores, clerks comment on his smile. In church, grandmothers fight over who gets to hold him. I'm pretty sure he's spoiled, even at this young age.

But it's not as though I'm without blame. If any-

Adriane

thing, I'm his enabler. If he fusses and my sister doesn't immediately rush to pick him up, I storm in like a SWAT team with toys, books, and blankets. Before he even thinks about crying, I'm there to hold him. And if he's out in a crowd, sleepily leaning his head on my sister's shoulder, I frown at people talking too loudly who might be keeping him from his afternoon nap. I, to be sure, have always "given him his heart's desire" (Psalm 21:2).

There's very little that he wants that he doesn't get, and I wonder sometimes if he knows it. Bang my spoon on the table, he no doubt thinks, and Mom hops up to get me another jar of vanilla custard dessert. Let out a disgruntled squawk as I start to tip over, and Dad's there to set me up again. Stick out my bottom lip, and Grandma's hands dart out with my favorite blankie. Grin coyly at the older ladies behind me in church, and they'll all let out giggles. Slobber on Pastor, and he'll rub my head and comment on my goofy hair until I laugh. What Oliver wants, Oliver gets.

I, however, remember very clearly a time when as a child I didn't get what I wanted. In fact, to this day, I give my mother a hard time about some play dough that I still contend is rightfully mine. I was on my way to the doctor as a nervous six-year-old, ready to get all the shots needed before attending school. If I didn't cry when the doctor poked me with needles, Mom promised to buy me some play dough. But this wasn't just any old play dough. It was a big set of three containers, each holding a primary-colored lump of that deliciously squishable goop. I'd had my eye on that prize for quite a while, so with my stomach in knots and my bottom lip stuck firmly between my teeth, I gritted out the visit to the doctor's office without shedding one little tear. And then, without batting an eye, my mom took me home. If I had known what the word meant, I would have described myself as incredulous. *No play dough?* My world had come to an obvious end. In my young mind, my mother's behavior was nothing short of shameful. I had no way of knowing that my poor mother, with her mind on what was in the refrigerator that she could use for supper and if she'd remembered to put the whites in the dryer, had simply forgotten her promise. Does that keep me from reminding her of

Adriane

it to this day? Quite the opposite. I wanted that play dough, and I should have gotten it!

Unfortunately, our craving for things doesn't change as we mature. As long as there's money in the checking account, we think we deserve whatever it takes to keep us happy. It can be as easy as getting a new pair of sandals to match last-year's capris or as superficial as wanting the latest pink cell phone. If we want it, we should get it.

Just because we want something doesn't mean He'll give it. It does mean, however, that our Lord understands and realizes what we really do need. Our hearts' desires are known to Him. God hears our prayers. He knows what we want. He understands our needs. He recognizes what's best for us, what will benefit us, and what we need most to hear.

This even carries over into a realm of things that can't be bought. If your best friend is dating a handsome guy who willingly goes shopping with her, it's clearly not fair. He should be with you instead. If a woman from down the street gets a seat on the school board, it's got to be a lack of education on the part of the voters. Your intellect is clearly superior. If your husband spends an entire Saturday afternoon playing basketball with your son instead of helping you around the house, it's obviously not right. You shouldn't be stuck inside all day doing laundry. And when your grandmother gives her antique teapot collection to your younger sister, well, that's just plain rude. She should have known you'd always liked it. If we want it, we deserve it, and when we don't get it, we're not amused.

But because we're busy drooling over new purses and lusting after leadership roles and yearning for more attention, we have failed to notice one thing: "the request of [our] lips" (v. 2) has not been denied us. We have been given Jesus, who is the fulfillment of all our requests, all of our needs, and all of our wants, although we may not realize it.

To be sure, this doesn't mean that because God *is* the answer He'll *give* us our answer. It's unlikely that He'll magically make our bodies model thin. He probably won't leave a brand-new pool in the backyard. He may not even give us perfect children who behave like angels in the grocery store. Just because we want

Adriane

something doesn't mean He'll give it. It does mean, however, that our Lord understands and realizes what we really do need. Our hearts' desires are known to Him. God hears our prayers. He knows what we want. He understands our needs. He recognizes what's best for us, what will benefit us, and what we need most to hear.

Although we may not be aware of it, God does give us our heart's desire. He doesn't withhold the requests of our lips that are in accordance with His will. And He certainly meets us with a multitude of rich blessings. Most of the time, these good things come in forms we don't even recognize, such as the parents He gives to love us, pastors to teach us, best friends to amuse us, and little babies to need us. He gives us chocolate cheesecake to fill us, minivans to transport us, three-bedroom ranches to shelter us, sweatshirts to warm us, and Dean Martin's music to soothe us. God gives us sun to cheer us, rain to sober us, sunsets to amaze us, and snow to delight us.

And believe it or not, God gives us even more. He provides us with His Word to teach us about our Savior. He uses His Word to guide us and to comfort us. And then He sends more. He provides Baptism to create faith and to forgive us our sins. He saves us from eternity in hell. He bestows on us the promise of time without end in heaven. But there is still more. He gives us His Holy Supper, Jesus' very body and blood, for the forgiveness of sins and to sustain us in the faith. He grants us absolution. He reassures us with His presence. Everything we need, He freely gives.

To put it simply, our heavenly Father has a point of view that we do not. He sees from the perspective of eternity. He understands what we need beyond this life. He gives us blessings whose wealth cannot be understood in terms of dollars or euros or yen. Instead, His gifts can be seen only through the lens of eternity, gifts that are crucial for our sanctification. If He knows we need it, it is ours.

Our Lord daily honors the superficial requests of our lips. He even gives us little things that we may not need but that can make our lives a little more pleasant—ceiling fans when we're

Adriane

89

feeling hot in the summer, chocolate chip cookie dough ice cream when we're feeling sad, hair color when we're feeling old, and vacations for when we're feeling exhausted. He meets us with more blessings than we can count. But at the end of the day, the only blessing that matters is the gift of Himself. Jesus is our heart's desire. He is the request of our lips. He is our richest blessing. And because of Him, we get exactly what we need.

Prayer: Dearest Lord Jesus, sometimes I am so distracted by this life that I lose sight of my life in You. I ask You to strengthen my faith and guide my thoughts and prayers by Your Holy Spirit so I want only what pleases and glorifies You. Keep me focused on Your cross and the promise of forgiveness and eternal life that are mine through You. In Your name. Amen.

Adriane

tuesday

Personal Study Questions: Psalm 21:2–5

1. Fittingly, the author of today's faith narrative applies verses 2–5 of the psalm to us, God's children. But before they applied to us, they applied to Jesus, our King. Because of what the Messiah did for us, we, too, can claim these blessings. When have you experienced the blessings described here in ways similar to those the faith narrative describes?

2. One hymn begins, "The head that once was crowned with thorns Is crowned with glory now" (*Lutheran Service Book* 532:1). What does the "crown" in verse 3 indicate?

3. When did Jesus "ask life" of the Father and receive it? What kind of life (v. 4)?

4. How does the salvation the Lord provides for us in the cross of His Son make the Messiah's glory great (v. 5)?

Adriane

Psalm 21:6–7

For You make him most blessed forever; You make him glad with the joy of Your presence. For the king trusts in the LORD; and through the steadfast love of the Most High he shall not be moved.

My Special Someone

Remember the last time you were in Wal-Mart? You were standing in the ten-items-or-less express lane with three simple things—maybe napkins, a yard of fabric for a craft project, and some mascara. You just wanted to run in, run out, and get home. You didn't want to see people you know. You didn't want to chat. You didn't want to browse. You didn't want to be bothered. You just wanted to get your stuff and go.

But it never works that way. That would be too easy. Instead, just as the woman in front of you began to place her items (of which there were more than ten, by the way) on the conveyor, her three-year-old son with the chocolate milk mustache began to throw a tantrum. And this was no small fit. Screaming, kicking, crying, threatening—he was doing it all. By the time she paid for her things, put them back in the cart, and placated him with the promise of a fast-food meal, the ten minutes you'd given yourself to dash in and out and to jump into your car had doubled. You could have gone through the self-checkout line, broken the scanner, sought an employee to punch in her key code to fix it, and then gone back to wait for a prescription to be filled in the amount of time it took this woman. *It's people like that,* you grumbled to yourself as you finally stomped past the smiling greeter, *who certainly do not make people* "glad with the joy of [their] presence" (v. 6).

Then again, you may have thought as you dashed in front of a teenager driving too quickly through the pedestrian zone, few people do. Your cranky next-door neighbor who gripes about how brown your lawn is surely doesn't make you happy. Your lazy mechanic who smokes more than a steamboat and speaks in jargon you can't understand doesn't. And neither does your son's irritable school librarian who snarls at innocent children.

Then, as you impatiently waited for an old couple to cross at the light, your still frustrated thoughts turn to family members. Not many of them make you happy with their presence. Your overly critical mother, your two jealous little sisters, and your conniving second cousin consistently do just the opposite. And don't get you started on your husband's parents. They're nowhere close to qualifying as joys in your mind.

At this very instant, however, you probably wouldn't make many people around you very cheerful either. But just stop for a moment and think. Think *hard.* While God gives you every person in your life as a gift, there is always at least one person—one parent, one friend, one mentor—who makes you happy just by being herself.

Adriane

For me, that person was my maternal grandmother. She had the ability to make me glad with the joy of her mere presence. She was the type of person people wanted to be near. It wasn't because she had a bubbly, outgoing personality. She didn't dazzle the world with her ability to talk about foreign policy or the effects of existentialism on modern-day culture. She never flew the space shuttle or ran for public office. She didn't have expensive clothes or a brand-new Cadillac in the garage. She never worked on saving the ozone, and she never volunteered with the Red Cross.

God doesn't give us just a taste of His blessings or only a smidgen of His presence. He goes all out. He rains down blessings on us like a thunderstorm in the mountains, although we are completely undeserving.

But she did do one thing: she made people glad when they were in her presence. She was a simple woman, content to raise her children, cook good meals, be involved at church, spoil her grandchildren, and get in her nightly walk around town. But her ability to be genuine in a quiet, sweet way was what made people love her.

I always adored being around her. For all outward appearances, she was a prim, meek, quiet school secretary. But to me, she was, as a radio personality would say, "More fun than a human being should be allowed to have." She belly danced. She giggled. She sang. She tickled, teased, loved, gave, hugged. She made me glad.

But certain times stand out more clearly than others. The times my sisters and I got to spend a weekend at her house were always the best. The fun usually began right after supper. The board game Aggravation was brought from the closet. Popcorn was popped. Miniature cans of cola were distributed. The laughter was plentiful. As the night wore on, she brought out homemade ice cream. Next was Yahtzee. Then, there were cookies. Finally, it was M&M's. She loved to see us full and happy, and we loved to oblige her.

On Saturday mornings, she was ready for us before we even got up. Powdered sugar donuts and grape juice, our standard Saturday-morning-at-Gram's-house fare, were already on the table, and cartoons were playing quietly in the background. She

Adriane

knew it made us happy, and that knowledge was all she needed to be content. She was happy, we were happy, and everyone was happy to be around one another.

Gram even went with us on most vacations. It wasn't that she went along because we felt obligated to take her. We didn't invite her because it made us look generous to our neighbors. We genuinely wanted her to join in the fun. We liked having her around. She added an extra dimension to our family that couldn't be replaced.

It wasn't just her family that enjoyed her presence. Most of the people in her small town knew she was something special. Friends stopped by her house every morning, knowing the coffee pot was already on and percolating. Church members knew they could call on her with a moment's notice to have cookie bars or a salad ready for a funeral luncheon. Neighbors counted on stopping to chat with her in their backyard after supper at night.

Her co-workers realized her warmth and kindness too. When she retired, dozens of teachers and staff members attended her party. Everyone regretted her leaving the school. Her quiet smile, her sweet charm, her homemade fudge, her delicious cinnamon rolls—each person had a different reason why they'd miss her. She made people glad just to be around her.

I tend to forget this, especially when I'm behind ill-mannered children in the checkout lane, but there is Someone who gladdens me even more than my grandmother. Someone who bestows on me even more blessings than my powdered-sugar-donut-and-M&M-gifting grandmother.

Not only does He *give* blessings, but He *is* the blessing. And while He makes us glad with His *presence*, He also cheers us by giving us *Himself*. But there's more.

We hurt our friends. We say rude things to our mothers. We antagonize our co-workers. We're hateful to our husbands or boy-friends. We're disrespectful to our children. We're wrong. We're mean. We're arrogant. We sin. Yet our Lord still forgives. He never stops.

In fact, He doesn't give us just a taste of His blessings or

Adriane

only a smidgen of His presence. He goes all out. He rains down blessings on us like a thunderstorm in the mountains, although we are completely undeserving. Once He gave Himself fully on the cross; now He gives us all the benefits of that cross in His Supper, in Baptism, and in His Holy Word. There's no half-heartedness on His part. He asks nothing in return. He is always giving, and we are always receiving. He makes it easy for us to be joyful in His presence. We are blessed, we are glad, and it truly is all because of Him.

Prayer: My Lord God, You have filled my life with blessings of all kinds. And I don't deserve any of it! Let me always be aware of Your blessings and, most of all, Your forgiveness in Christ Jesus. Let me be refreshed daily in baptismal grace by Your gifts of Word and Sacrament. Teach me to love others as You love me through Your Son. In Jesus' name I pray. Amen.

Adriane

Personal Study Questions:
Psalm 21:6–7

1. Verse 6 can be translated in two ways:
   "You make him most blessed forever."
   "You make him a source of blessing forever."

   a. How are each true of the psalm's author, King David?

   b. How are each true of King Jesus?

2. In whose presence do you almost always feel glad in the ways described in today's faith narrative? Why?

3. Reread verse 7.

   a. In what ways was this true of David?

   b. In what ways is it true of Jesus?

   c. In what ways is it true of *you*?

Adriane

Psalm 21:8–12

Your hand will find out all Your enemies; Your right hand will find out those who hate You. You will make them as a blazing oven when You appear. The LORD will swallow them up in His wrath, and fire will consume them. You will destroy their descendants from the earth, and their offspring from among the children of man. Though they plan evil against You, though they devise mischief, they will not succeed. For You will put them to flight; You will aim at their faces with Your bows.

The Enemy

I don't want to have any enemies. Nor do I want to think anyone hates me. In fact, I'd much rather assume that they don't. After all, I'm nice to people. I smile. I endure hugs from relatives I don't like. I try not to be rude when the airline loses my luggage. I make chitchat with older women. I ask the grocery store clerk in the checkout line how her day is going. I'm pleasant to my teachers. I listen to my parents. I keep in touch with old friends. In general, I try not

Adriane

to give people any reason to hate me.

But just because I want others to like me doesn't mean that I don't dislike them. In fact, I find it very easy to think poorly of people. For instance, in college I had a rival. She was a sister English literature student, although if she had majored in being annoying and minored in causing frustration, I could have at least respected her honesty. She was the kind of person who always did the extra credit even when she clearly didn't need to. She went to coffee shop poetry readings just so she could flaunt her critical analysis skills in front of the class. She spent long hours discussing the merits of assonance and alliteration in couplet phrasing with the professor. She had a tendency to say things like "When you love Italian poetry as much as I do, you don't even notice hendecasyllable verse after a while!" And as if that wasn't painful enough, lunch-table conversation often centered on a recent reading of her favorite transcendental author the rest of us didn't even try to understand.

I really didn't like her. I got mad just by seeing her in the hall. Even hearing her name made me roll my eyes. She probably never even knew that I couldn't stand her. But that didn't keep me from considering her my enemy nonetheless.

She never did anything to me personally. She didn't slash my tires. She didn't steal money from me. She didn't spread nasty rumors. She didn't "plan evil" against me or "devise mischief" to ruin my life (v. 11). She didn't even talk to me very much. But she annoyed me just by being herself. I found myself wishing she would just pack up, move, and transfer to another school far, far away so I wouldn't have to listen to her or hear her or think about her.

To put the best construction on the situation, I wasn't praying for her death. I didn't actually want God to scoop her up, kicking and screaming, and toss her into a huge gas-burning oven. When she and her fiancé were married, I didn't pray that God would kill their children. I didn't want her parents to be obliterated by God's wrath. Now that I think about it, maybe she wasn't much of an enemy after all.

But I do have enemies—actual, real-life, tangible, anger-filled enemies. They hate me. They really do want me to die. It's not that I've been rude to them. I haven't ignored them. I never did anything to hurt them. But that doesn't stop them from hoping for my demise. They hate me for a completely different reason: because I have been baptized.

So it is that God alone helps us to forgive. He teaches us how to pray. He shows us how to love. He keeps an eye on the sparrows. He takes care of us. And on the Last Day, when He calls us out of the grave and to Himself, no terrorist or torturer or tempter will be able to stop Him.

This may sound like bad news for me, but it's just as serious a situation for you. If they hate me for being a Christian, they abhor you too. They're disgusted by the fact that you go to church. They detest that you read the Scriptures. They loathe your desire to receive the Lord's Supper. They despise every minute you spend in Bible class. And if they could keep you from your nightly devotions with your family, they would do that too.

These are your enemies and mine, and they are real. They aren't just pretentious English majors. They're not just annoying. They're dangerous, and they hate you—and they hate Christ even more. They despise everything about Him. They reject His gift of grace. They reject His forgiveness. They reject Him.

And yet, just like I didn't actually want something bad to happen to my college archenemy, you and I can still somehow find it hard to pray that "The Lord will swallow them up in His wrath, and fire will consume them" (v. 9). It seems so harsh, so cruel, so final.

But God's anger and His wrath are very real. They are no joke. The verse "If anyone has no love for the Lord, let him be accursed" (1 Corinthians 16:22) is no weak threat. God has promised that He will execute judgment on those who oppose Him. These enemies of yours are really enemies of God's. They have rejected Him, rejected His Son, and reject those who by faith believe. The Judgment Day will be no picnic for them.

That leaves us with bad news and good news. The bad news is that we are just as deserving of this wrath as those who act on their hatred of Christ. We have sinned too. We have been jealous of our co-worker's new three-car garage. We've gotten mad about

Adriane

our sister's comments on our hairstyle. We are easily perturbed with our kids' lack of respect. So while we may not bomb churches or torture pastors or kill small children, we are still guilty.

But the good news is even better. God has already taken out His vengeance on someone else. It was anger meant for you and for me. It was rightfully ours. We deserved it. Instead, He placed all His wrath on Christ, and we go scot-free. He calls us sinners out on the carpet, but He forgives our trespasses. He despises our disbelief, but He hears, "Father, forgive them, for they know not what they do" (Luke 23:34). He sees our faults, but He assures us that the cross of Christ has secured love and forgiveness for us. We are safe. We are not His enemies.

You and I, in turn, cannot forgive our Father's enemies on our own. We cannot excuse murderers, torturers, and persecutors of Christians by our own power. Only Christ can do that. He alone gives us the ability to "Love your enemies and pray for those who persecute you" (Matthew 5:44). He endured God's wrath while on the cross. So it is that He alone helps us to forgive. He teaches us how to pray. He shows us how to love. He keeps an eye on the sparrows. He takes care of us. And on the Last Day, when He calls us out of the grave and to Himself, no terrorist or torturer or tempter will be able to stop Him.

Prayer: Dear Jesus, I don't deserve what You've done for me. By nature, I'm Your enemy. No matter how hard I try to do what's right, I still sin. And still, You love me. Still, You forgive me. Thank You, Jesus, for taking the punishment for my sin, for dying for me. Teach me to . . . (here add your own petitions). I ask in Your precious name. **Amen.**

Adriane

thursday

Personal Study Questions: Psalm 21:8–12

1. Like a mother defending her children from a fierce enemy, the Lord comes to our rescue. Think about a time someone came to your defense when you were helpless. How did it give you comfort and confidence? How does knowing Jesus' rescue, His promised defense of you, multiply the comfort and confidence you just described?

2. Our enemies were sin, Satan, hell, and death. How did the Lord fulfill verses 8–12 for us? How does this give you peace now and hope for your future?

3. Do we sing the Lord's praises because of the wonderful musical talent we possess and can share with Him or for some other reason? Explain, based on the faith narrative.

Psalm 21:13

Be exalted, O LORD, in Your strength!
We will sing and praise Your power.

A Song in the Air

I'm not a good singer. To be perfectly frank, I put the *noise* in "Make a joyful noise to the LORD" (Psalm 100:1). If He'd have said, "Make a harmonic, perfectly pitched, pleasing-to-the-ear, musical dramatization to the Lord," I'd be severely out of luck.

It's not that I sound like a dying walrus or a hungry bull moose. Crystal doesn't break when I sing. Neighborhood dogs can still sleep peacefully if I'm humming. Bach isn't rolling over in his grave. So I'm not that bad. It's just that I'm not good.

But I know good singers. In fact, I've known more good ones than bad. My parents are good singers. I remember leaning on my dad in church, too young to read the hymns, but still fascinated by the way his chest would rumble as he sang bass. Mom can harmonize, and the two of them together sound pretty good.

My aunt is an amazing singer too. In fact, she's a professionally trained soprano. When I was little, she was my piano teacher.

That beautiful music serves God and His Word. It communicates the certainty of what He has done for us in Christ. It conveys the Gospel through song. It tells us of God's forgiveness. It reminds us of His death on the cross. It repeats the story of our salvation.

Not every child gets to play "Twinkle, Twinkle, Little Star" as accompaniment to an opera singer. We gave a concert once at Christmas for our whole family. I played the piano; she turned pages and sang. No one even noticed I was there, and rightly so. Her crisp, clear voice commanded everyone's attention.

My best friend in high school was an alto in the choir. I was a disgruntled soprano who wanted to be an alto. We stood next to each other a lot, mainly so we could talk, but also so I could learn the alto part by listening to her. She tried, but I never caught on. Like I said, I'm just not good.

My college roommate was a music fanatic. She won awards in state competitions. She played piano like Mozart and was invited to be in the college choir. When she started taking organ lessons, I decided to take organ lessons too. This was fun at first, but after she began playing better than our instructor, I didn't want her to hear me practice anymore. After all, if it was musical, she could master it. There was no competition from me.

There were only two days out of the year when my roommate set aside her strict musicality. On the last day of each semester, the choir director invited all willing attendees to the front of the chapel. There, in celebration of the semester's end, they would attempt to sing the "Hallelujah Chorus" with no practice or preparation. My roommate and I would stake out the back pew of the chapel. Each time, we would giggle for a good ten minutes while the musically challenged students fumbled their way through the piece. Each time, it sounded absolutely horrible. Each time, we showed up just to hear how awful it would sound. Those were the

Adriane

only times she ever condoned bad music.

Now I have a new favorite singer to listen to. My friend at church has a beautiful voice. She was asked to sing in a unique Baroque choir, one of only a few in the world. Her obvious talent is made even more amazing by the fact that she always says, "Ohhhhh, I'm not that good," and really believes it.

Simply put, in every stage of my life, I've had my own personal expert musician to sit by in chapel or choir or church. Somehow, being surrounded by talented singers makes it easier for me to accept that I'll never sound like Julie Andrews in *The Sound of Music*.

Not everyone sings. Not everyone sings well. Not everyone enjoys singing. And to be honest, sometimes we just don't feel like it. We put on the music of Michael Bublé or James Blunt. We curl up on the couch, head on a pillow. We don't want to talk. We don't want to sing. We just want to hear something slow and somber and sad.

But sometimes we *are* in the mood to sing. If Frank Sinatra is crooning on the car radio, you may join along. If you're vacuuming, and the Beatles are keeping you company, you jump in and accompany them. If your three-year-old is singing his ABCs, you bob your head in time to the music and help him out.

Thankfully, our Lord doesn't close His ears when we sing. He doesn't require that you or I sound remotely like Judy Garland or Dinah Shore or Ella Fitzgerald. He's not concerned whether you can hit the high notes or sing "Happy Birthday" to your grandmother with perfect pitch. It isn't about the sound of your voice. It isn't about what part you sing or whether you can sight-read a difficult hymn on demand. Ability is unimportant. Tone is irrelevant.

What *is* important is Christ. He is to be the focus of all our praise. He is the one about whom we sing. He is the one who causes us to praise Him in the first place. So whether you warble or bellow or harmonize, sing of Christ. Thank Him for His mercy. Praise Him for His faithfulness. Speak of His grace. With the psalmist, say, "But I will sing of Your strength; I will sing aloud of

Adriane

Your steadfast love in the morning. For You have been to me a fortress and a refuge in the day of my distress" (Psalm 59:16).

Go ahead and repeat the liturgy you sing each Sunday in church. There your heavenly Father comes to you in His Word set to music. He forgives your sins. He speaks to you. The angels and Abraham and archangels and your sister who died in the faith and the company of heaven and King David sing with you. Together, across time, you praise your Creator, singing back to Him what He first spoke to you.

That beautiful music serves God and His Word. It communicates the certainty of what He has done for us in Christ. It conveys the Gospel through song. It tells us of God's forgiveness. It reminds us of His death on the cross. It repeats the story of our salvation.

So grab your hymnal and find "A Mighty Fortress." Sing with your family around the piano on Christmas Eve. Belt out a stanza or two in the shower. Shout out the "Gloria in Excelsis." Help your preschooler memorize a Sunday School song. Practice a hymn each time you open a window on your Advent calendar or as part of your Lenten devotions. Better yet, pick one to memorize with your family before prayers each evening.

Your heavenly Father loves you. He has forgiven you. He has a place in heaven with your name on it. He has saved you through His Son. So sing. Jesus Christ is reason enough.

Prayer: Dear Lord Jesus Christ, let my life be a song of praise and thanksgiving to You. Let my heart and my mouth sing of Your righteousness. Let me join in a hymn of worship to You, for Your sake. Amen.

Adriane

Friday

Personal Study Questions: Psalm 21:13

1. We often praise the Lord for His mercy, His forgiveness, His unending love.

   a. Do you praise Him as often for His power as for His mercy? Why or why not?

   b. For what reasons are you glad He is almighty, all-powerful, in addition to being compassionate and forgiving?

2. The Lord cannot get any stronger or more glorious. He already is both almighty and infinite in glory. In what way, then, do we pray that His glory be "magnified" and that He be "exalted"?

Adriane

Group Bible Study for Week 3
Psalm 21

1. Which devotional reading for this week touched your heart most deeply? Explain.

2. In one sense, Psalm 21 describes the earthly reign of King David in Israel one thousand years before Jesus was born in Bethlehem. Which words and phrases illustrate this?

3. In another sense, this psalm outlines the work of the Messiah, the Savior long promised by God to rescue fallen humanity from our sins, from Satan, and from eternal death. What words and phrases illustrate this?

4. In a third sense, the psalm describes us—the royal children of the heavenly King (Ephesians 1:3–14).

   a. How does Psalm 21 outline in broad strokes some of the blessings we have inherited in Jesus, our Savior?

   b. What further details does Ephesians 1 add as it describes our inheritance?

5. Read John 12:20–28. Compare it with Psalm 21:2–7.

   a. The Messiah's glory did not come as an afterthought in the plan of God. What evidence in the psalm proves that Jesus' "glory" was part of that plan from all eternity?

   b. How does the passage from John make it clear that the cross *was* and *is* the Messiah's glory?

   c. How does the psalm itself hint at this?

   d. How do both the psalm and the account in John's Gospel indicate that the freedom from sin and death Jesus won for us would also form a significant part of the Messiah's glory?

6. How do verses such as 1 Corinthians 15:43; 2 Thessalonians 2:14; and 2 Timothy 2:10, which speak of the glory God gives us in Christ, describe the glory that is and will be ours?

7. Now read John 17:20–23.

    a. What specific blessings does Jesus ask His Father to give in this portion of His High Priestly Prayer?

    b. How does the psalm foreshadow or hint at this?

    c. Consider the fact that Jesus shares His very own glory with us (John 17:22)! How is Psalm 21 an appropriate hymn of praise in response to the salvation we have received?

8. Pray this psalm together as you conclude today's session.

Week Four

Psalm 45

[1] My heart overflows with a pleasing theme;
I address my verses to the king;
my tongue is like the pen of a ready scribe.

[2] You are the most handsome of the sons of men;
grace is poured upon Your lips;
therefore God has blessed You forever.

[3] Gird Your sword on Your thigh, O mighty one,
in Your splendor and majesty!

[4] In Your majesty ride out victoriously
for the cause of truth and meekness and righteousness;
let Your right hand teach You awesome deeds!

[5] Your arrows are sharp
in the heart of the king's enemies;
the peoples fall under You.

[6] Your throne, O God, is forever and ever.
The scepter of Your kingdom is a scepter of uprightness;
[7] You have loved righteousness and hated wickedness.
Therefore God, Your God, has anointed You
with the oil of gladness beyond Your companions;

⁸ Your robes are all fragrant with myrrh and aloes and cassia.
From ivory palaces stringed instruments make You glad;
⁹ daughters of kings are among Your ladies of honor;
at Your right hand stands the queen in gold of Ophir.

¹⁰ Hear, O daughter, and consider, and incline your ear:
forget your people and your father's house,

¹¹ and the king will desire your beauty.
Since He is your lord, bow to Him.

¹² The people of Tyre will seek your favor with gifts,
the richest of the people.

¹³ All glorious is the princess in her chamber, with robes interwoven
with gold.

¹⁴ In many-colored robes she is led to the king,
with her virgin companions following behind her.

¹⁵ With joy and gladness they are led along
as they enter the palace of the king.

¹⁶ In place of Your fathers shall be Your sons;
You will make them princes in all the earth.

¹⁷ I will cause Your name to be remembered in all generations;
therefore nations will praise You forever and ever.

Diane Grebing

Psalm 45:1–2

My heart overflows with a pleasing theme;
I address my verses to the king; my tongue
is like the pen of a ready scribe.

Praising the Love
of Our Lives

"Hello, Diane? This is Nancy. Have I got some news for you!"

Always happy to hear from my best friend from college, I quickly replied, "Really? Tell me more."

"I'm engaged! His name is Bill. He's the most wonderful man! He's kind and caring, smart and quick-witted, *very* handsome . . . he's the love of my life! I've never been happier!"

"Wow, Nancy! Congratulations! Your fiancé sounds great! I can't wait to meet him!"

It's been more than twenty years since Nancy called with her joyful news. Although I wasn't able to see her face during our phone conversation, her loving and praising words for her husband-to-be let me know the happiness she felt in her heart.

Perhaps you, too, have heard similar words from your best friend. Perhaps you've heard them from your daughter or from another family member. You may have even used similar words yourself when describing your own husband.

Experiencing the love of another makes our hearts "overflow." When we've found the love of our life, we want to tell everyone our good news. At times like this, descriptive words about our loved one flow joyfully and readily from our tongue.

The tongue of the author of Psalm 45 readily praises Jesus, our King. The psalmist gushes in verse 2, "You are the most handsome of the sons of men; grace is poured upon Your lips; therefore God has blessed You forever." These words express admiration of our Lord's presence and His prominence. They profess heartfelt thankfulness for the undeserved love and forgiveness our Savior daily shows. They acknowledge that God has eternally blessed Jesus.

Throughout the entire Book of Psalms, we read similar songs of overflowing praise:

✻ How great are Your works, O LORD! Your thoughts are very deep! Psalm 92:5

✻ Great are the works of the LORD, studied by all who delight in them. Full of splendor and majesty is His work, and His righteousness endures forever. Psalm 111:2–3

✻ O come, let us sing to the LORD; let us make a joyful noise to the rock of our salvation! Let us come into His

Diane

113

presence with thanksgiving; let us make a joyful noise to Him with songs of praise! For the LORD is a great God, and a great King above all gods. Psalm 95:1–3

✳ The LORD is high above all nations, and His glory above the heavens! Psalm 113:4

✳ Great is the LORD, and greatly to be praised, and His greatness is unsearchable. Psalm 145:3

Our Lord Jesus *is* great! In fact, no one is greater. Jesus willingly left His throne in heaven to become a humble human. He showed the greatest love ever when He willingly suffered and died on our behalf so we could be saved from our sins. Through Jesus' death and resurrection, we have eternal life and God's forgiveness. By His saving love, Jesus has brought us back to God. Through Jesus, we are chosen to be "a royal priesthood, a holy nation, a people for His own possession" (1 Peter 2:9).

Jesus never lets us down. The Love of our life is perfect, without sin (2 Corinthians 5:21). Actively involved in our lives, He invites us to lay down our burdens on Him so He can take them upon Himself (Matthew 11:28).

Think of it: Jesus did this all for *you!* Jesus has saved you from eternal death. He has cleansed you from your sins. He has reunited you with God. He has claimed you as His own beloved child. Jesus has done all this for you not because you've earned it or deserved it by your own actions. He has done all this for you only because of the grace for you that is "poured on" His lips.

Jesus' love and grace for us is constant and eternal. He never changes (Hebrews 13:8). Unfortunately, the same is not true concerning our human relationships. If I called my friend Nancy today, here's how our conversation might transpire:

"Hello, Nancy? It's Diane. We haven't talked for a while and I just thought I'd check in. How's everything with you?"

"Oh, Diane, (sigh) it's so good to hear from you!" (Pauses and sighs again.) "I've been running myself ragged. After teaching all day, my evenings are filled with taking the kids to piano lessons and swimming lessons and ball games. Then there's cooking, cleaning, laundry . . . "

"I understand, Nancy. It sure is a good thing you've got Bill to give you a hand."

"Bill!" (Another pause and another sigh.) "He comes home after work, plops in the recliner, and doesn't lift a finger, much less a hand, to help me."

Our Prince Charmings aren't always so charming, are they? You could say that the initial gushing admiration Nancy expressed for Bill has temporarily dried to a slow trickle. Despite our love for our husbands, daily tasks and challenges bring out their imperfections (and ours).

But not so with Jesus. Jesus never lets us down. The Love of our life is perfect, without sin (2 Corinthians 5:21). Actively involved in our lives, He invites us to lay down our burdens on Him so He can take them upon Himself (Matthew 11:28). His Word directs us to cast "all your anxieties on Him, because He cares for you" (1 Peter 5:8). When we are in trouble, we can call upon Him, and He will answer and help us (Psalm 50:15).

Jesus' caring love touches our hearts and makes them swell with gratitude and praise. In love with our Lord through faith in Him, our hearts beat faster with excitement. Stirred by His grace and compassion, we tell everyone the good news about our relationship with Him.

Left on our own, we can't praise Jesus like the psalmist. Our own words may be hesitant instead of freely flowing. But, enabled by the Holy Spirit, we can sing heartfelt praises to Him. Ephesians 5:18 says, "Be filled with the Spirit, addressing one another in psalms and hymns and spiritual songs, singing and making melody to the Lord with your heart." By the Gospel, the Holy Spirit gives us the wonderful saving knowledge of Jesus in which we can trust and rejoice. By the power of the Holy Spirit, we are filled with all joy and peace, and we overflow with hope (Romans 15:13).

Empowered by the Holy Spirit, imagine making this phone call:

"Hello, girlfriend! Have I got some news for you! I've found

Diane

115

the love of my life. He's kind, caring, loving, forgiving . . . in fact, He's perfect in every way. He's sacrificed everything for me. He has promised to be with me forever, even into eternity. The name of my love is Jesus. I can't wait for you to meet Him!"

Prayer: Dearest Jesus, You are our perfect King. In You, we find all joy and delight. Your love puts a new song in our hearts and makes them overflow with love and praise for You. By the power of the Holy Spirit, help us share Your love with others as we tell them how much You mean to us. Let words of admiration for You flow from our lips. Give us the overflowing desire to share You with others. We pray all this in Your name. Amen.

Diane

monday

Personal Study Questions: Psalm 45:1–2

1 Think about a time a Prince Charming charmed you less than you had hoped. What created your disappointment?

2. As Korah's sons begin their love song, they tell us that their hearts overflow. Recall a time your heart brimmed over with emotion. What brought that on?

3. Have you ever experienced that kind of overwhelming love as you read Scripture, prayed with God's people, or knelt at the Lord's Table? What brought that on?

4. What might it mean that "grace is poured upon [Jesus'] lips" (v. 2)?

Diane

Psalm 45:3–5

In Your majesty ride out victoriously
for the cause of truth and meekness
and righteousness.

A Knight in Shining Armor

s a child, I longed for adventure. Enraptured by episodes of *Superman* and *Batman*, I, too, wanted to be rescued from danger by a hero with a cape. But my ordinary life growing up in the suburbs did not exactly lend itself to adventure. So instead, I made up my own with the help of a collection of glass animals and other figurines from the top of my bookcase.

Depending upon the adventure, the yellow blown-

Diane

118

glass stork with the bright red beak purchased on a Florida vacation might become hopelessly lost in the mountains of a faraway land. The porcelain princess whose skirt was adorned with the November birthstone might be kidnapped by the plastic orange-haired troll from the local dime store. The tiny black glass seal from the aquarium might be clinging for his life on the edge of a glacier (top of the bookshelf) trying to escape the clutches of the carved wooden bear from the north woods of Wisconsin. But no matter what character from my collection was in trouble, the rescuer was always the same: a small plastic stallion with a black flowing mane that my mom had given me after a good report card in the second grade. Just when the lost, kidnapped, or threatened character believed all was hopeless, in would race the plastic stallion, prepared to save him or her from the plight.

When I outgrew these playtimes, I continued to enjoy novels and movies that centered on the battle of good versus evil, especially those that involved "a knight in shining armor"-type character who rushed in at the appropriate time to save the day. While not wanting to be pictured as a helpless "damsel in distress," it was an exciting thought for me to be rescued from danger and to be cared for by a strong, handsome man riding in on a powerful stallion. This "knight in shining armor" imagery also became a component in my dreams about marriage. Like many young women, I waited to be swept off my feet by a man who would be my majestic hero. God eventually led me to a man who became my wonderful, caring husband. But I soon discovered that he is no knight in shining armor, nor am I a beautiful princess. And I still longed for someone to rescue me from danger, problems, and worries.

Much of the distress and danger we daily face is of our own making. Poorly made decisions, angry words and thoughts, discontent, and jealousy are but a few of the things we feel and express that cause us misery. Other distress and danger comes from sources outside of us. Violence, anger, and hatred are but a few of the poisonous arrows slung at us by others that harm us physically and emotionally.

Diane

The dangers that we damsels in distress face are the result of sin and Satan's evil actions in the world. Scripture says: "Be sober-minded; be watchful. Your adversary the devil prowls around like a roaring lion, seeking someone to devour" (1 Peter 5:8). These are frightening words. Satan's desire isn't just to temporarily bruise or injure us. Satan's desire isn't just to break our hearts for a time or to give us troubles that are short-lived. No, Satan wants to *devour* us. The devil delights in nothing less than to chew us up, tear us apart, and swallow us whole—forever. He will use any means to do so.

Daily, Satan attacks us physically and emotionally with well-recognized dangers: discord in our marriages and with our children, disagreements and disconnection from friends, worries about jobs and finances, and concerns and fears about local and worldwide events. These dangers can make us unhappy, ill, doubtful, isolated, and hopeless. They can cause us to take our focus off of God's supreme power and strength.

These words are no fantasy! They are no fairy tale! They are the wonderful truth! So rejoice and be confident in your daily life adventure! Jesus is your Savior, your hero, your true knight in shining armor for whom you have been longing!

Even more dangerous are the subtle ways Satan attacks us. The devil pummels and wages war on our souls with eternally deadly dangers that he often hides in innocent-looking packages. These dangers include misinterpreting God's true Word and combining it with worldly philosophies that make us think we can rescue ourselves. Satan's tricks cast doubt into our minds as to whether God truly loves us. These dangers, engineered by Satan, try to strip us from the arms of our true and loving God. They lead us to depend on things of the world instead of on God's everlasting, heavenly gifts and His loving all-powerful strength. Satan's taunts, although they may look and sound truthful, are instead deadly bombs of lies and destruction that seek to send us to a place of eternal darkness and suffering.

This is definitely not the adventure I signed up for! We cry out with the psalmists, "Lord God, rescue us!"

Diane

Thankfully, our loving God provides a happily-ever-after ending to this earthly story. Psalm 45:3–5 tells of God's rescue plan for us that includes a true knight in shining armor. Our knight's name is Jesus. Girded with the sword of His Word, which is the "word of life" to a "crooked and twisted generation" (Philippians 2:15–16), Jesus rides out "victoriously" in "splendor and majesty" "for the cause of truth and meekness and righteousness." Jesus is indeed the rescuer we need.

Jesus is "the way, and the truth, and the life" (John 14:6). He "came into the world to save sinners" (1 Timothy 1:15). Jesus came from heaven to be our humble servant. He told His disciples, "But whoever would be great among you must be your servant, and whoever would be first among you must be your slave, even as the Son of Man came not to be served but to serve, and to give His life as a ransom for many" (Matthew 20:26–28). Through Jesus' death and resurrection, we receive the gift of being made right with God from our sins. By Jesus' "obedience the many will be made righteous" (Romans 5:19).

Jesus' actions on our behalf saved us from the deadly intent of the devil. Jesus' sharp "arrows" (v. 5) cut to the heart of the evil one. Through His death on the cross, Jesus destroyed "the one who has the power of death, that is, the devil" (Hebrews 2:14). Through His resurrection, Jesus victoriously crushed Satan's death grip on us forever. "But thanks be to God, who gives us the victory through our Lord Jesus Christ" (1 Corinthians 15:57).

Satan knows that Jesus has defeated him. Jesus descended into hell to proclaim His victory over him (Colossians 2:15). Although Satan knows he is defeated, he continues to use his evil powers to try to get us away from God. While that's scary and despicable, Jesus, our Savior, assures us in His Word of His constant love and protection for us: "My sheep hear My voice, and I know them, and they follow Me. I give them eternal life, and they will never perish, and no one will snatch them out of My hand" (John 10:27–28). Further assurance is found in Romans 8:38–39: "neither death nor life, nor angels nor rulers, nor things present nor things to come, nor powers, nor height nor depth, nor any-

Diane

thing else in all creation, will be able to separate us from the love of God in Christ Jesus our Lord." On Judgment Day, Jesus will return and will lock Satan in the dungeon of hell forever. We, His bride the Church, will live forever in peace and in His everlasting glory.

My dear sister in Christ, these words are no fantasy! They are no fairy tale! They are the wonderful truth! So rejoice and be confident in your daily life adventure! Jesus is your Savior, your hero, your true knight in shining armor for whom you have been longing! Delight in Him and in His rescuing love.

Prayer: Dearest Savior, our hearts overflow with love for You! We thank You for rescuing us from the clutches of sin, death, and Satan through Your death on the cross and Your resurrection from the grave. Whenever we face dark dangers here on earth, help us to rely only on You and Your power, majesty, and strength. Remind us always of the safety we find in You and You alone. Be near us, Lord Jesus, forever. In Your name we pray. Amen.

Diane

122

tuesday

Personal Study Questions:
Psalm 45:3–5

1. How do the words of Psalm 45:3–5 suggest the rescue fantasies today's faith narrative describes?

2. How do these verses accurately reflect what Jesus has done for you?

3. "My dear sister in Christ, these words are no fantasy! They are no fairy tale! They are the wonderful truth!" So today's faith narrative reminds us.

   a. When do you rest most easily in this truth? When do you find it hardest to believe?

   b. How might rehearsing these verses often and perhaps even committing them to memory create increasing confidence and hope in your heart?

Diane

Psalm 45:6–7

*Therefore God, Your God, has anointed You with the
oil of gladness beyond Your companions. Psalm 45:7*

Madeover for Him

Growing up, I remember well what happened in my house each weekday somewhere around 4:30 p.m. At this appointed time, my mother would go into the bathroom, wash the day's grime off her face, and adorn herself with a bit of powder and lipstick. She would then disappear into her bedroom and shortly thereafter emerge wearing clean clothes, looking refreshed and renewed. At 5:00 p.m., the back door would open, and my father would come home from work. My mother would greet him with a kiss, and so our evening would begin.

Not being into makeup and glamour, it took me a

Diane

long time to understand and appreciate why my mom took the time for this mini-makeover every day. I eventually realized that she did it because she loved her husband. Although my father loved her no matter how she looked, she always wanted to look her very best for him.

My mother continued this ritual of love for my father her entire life, even as her body became ravaged by cancer. At the time of her illness, often too weak to trek to the bathroom just to apply makeup, she kept her lipstick and compact beside her recliner, ready for use. My mother's use of makeup was not a sign of vanity. It was something she did to set herself aside and to make herself special for her husband.

Psalm 45:7 tells how kings in Bible times were set apart and made special for service to God and to His people. Kings, priests, and sometimes prophets were prepared for the duties of their position through the ceremony of *anointing*. When anointed, a specially prepared holy oil was poured over the individual's head as a sign that he was now set apart to serve God. Aaron was anointed in this way to be Israel's priest (Exodus 29:7). Saul, Israel's first king, was anointed by Samuel to reign over God's people (1 Samuel 10:1). After Saul was rejected by God because of his disobedience, David was anointed by Samuel to replace Saul (1 Samuel 16:12–13). When a person was anointed, he was consecrated to holy service. The Spirit of God would enter each man, empowering him to serve God.

Jesus, ruler over all, reigns supreme on His throne over all things and beings, including the angels (Hebrews 1:4–9). He is the fulfillment of this psalm: our perfect and eternal King. He is anointed by God with "the oil of gladness beyond Your companions" (v. 7). From the time God promised Adam and Eve a Savior (Genesis 3:15), Jesus was set apart to serve His heavenly Father and us.

As a very young child, Jesus was recognized by people from far-off lands as special and supreme to any earthly ruler. Wise Men from the East offered to Him the kingly gifts of gold, frankincense, and myrrh as they bowed down and worshiped Him

Diane

(Matthew 2:11). At the beginning of His public ministry, Jesus told those in the synagogue at Nazareth, "The Spirit of the Lord is upon Me, because He has anointed Me to proclaim good news to the poor. He has sent Me to proclaim liberty to the captives and recovering of sight to the blind, to set at liberty those who are oppressed" (Luke 4:18). "God anointed Jesus of Nazareth with the Holy Spirit and with power. He went about doing good and healing all who were oppressed by the devil, for God was with Him" (Acts 11:38). Jesus was set apart by God to set us free from our sins through His death and resurrection. He set Himself aside to come to earth as a man and to serve and suffer for us. He is the Christ, the Messiah, the Anointed One. Jesus is anointed with the "oil of gladness" to be our Prophet, Priest, and King.

Baptism is no outer makeup that merely covers our blemishes. Baptism is a total inner and outer makeover that removes the blemishes of sin and re-creates us as new creations in Him.

My mom was so privileged in her life to have a much greater makeover than her daily makeup application could have ever achieved. Jesus set her aside as His anointed one without the use of powder or lipstick. Jesus set her aside through the spiritual makeover of Baptism. Combined with God's Word, the water of Baptism became my mother's "oil of gladness." When the water and Word washed over her, she was cleansed from her sins and filled with the Holy Spirit. "But when the goodness and loving kindness of God our Savior appeared, He saved us, not because of works done by us in righteousness, but according to His own mercy, by the washing of regeneration and renewal of the Holy Spirit, whom He poured out on us richly through Jesus Christ our Savior, so that being justified by His grace we might become heirs according to the hope of eternal life" (Titus 3:4–7). In Baptism, my mother was refreshed, renewed, set aside, chosen by Christ to belong to Him and to serve Him forever. In the eyes of Jesus, my mother is eternally beautiful and never in need of makeup, for her spiritual makeover was made complete in Him at her Baptism.

Just like my mother, Jesus has willingly anointed us to be His through our Baptism. Despite knowing all of our blemishes

Diane

and imperfections that we try to cover up, Jesus loves us so much that He died for us, rose for us, and lives for us. Anointed by Baptism's water and His Word, we delight in Jesus' daily tender and rich care for us, as a loving groom takes care of his bride. We receive His forgiveness for our sins. He fills our hearts with joy and gladness. He welcomes us to kneel before His throne to partake of His marvelous blessings of forgiveness, grace, and love.

Jesus, our King, has chosen us and has set us apart to belong to Him, to be a part of His kingdom, and to be "His people, and the sheep of His pasture" (Psalm 100:3). "And it is God who establishes us with you in Christ, and has anointed us, and who has also put His seal on us and given us His Spirit in our hearts as a guarantee" (2 Corinthians 1:21–22). We are marked by Jesus as His own. Baptism is no outer makeup that merely covers our blemishes. Baptism is a total inner and outer makeover that removes the blemishes of sin and re-creates us as new creations in Him.

God's Word puts it this way: "Christ loved the church and gave Himself up for her, that He might sanctify her, having cleansed her by the washing of water with the word, so that He might present the church to Himself in splendor, without spot or wrinkle or any such things, that she might be holy and without blemish" (Ephesians 5:25–27). As part of His chosen Church, His bride, we are set aside in Christ to love and honor Him as the One who does everything for us. Jesus sets us free from sin, death, and Satan. Jesus gives us the sure and certain hope of eternal life. Jesus gives us comfort, strength, and courage.

In the end, no earthly makeup could cover the physical damage that my mother's sickness caused. Despite the fact that eventually the cancer took her physical life, through faith in Jesus, my mom knew she belonged to Him and nothing could take her away from His love. Today my mother is in heaven with her heavenly Bridegroom, Jesus. She lives now in His perfect peace. Someday, she will experience one more makeover: this time a physical one that will give her a new, glorious body but that will require no makeup, only the Savior's loving hand.

The next time you look in the mirror as you apply your pow-

Diane

der or lipstick, rejoice that by the power of the Holy Spirit, you have already received the perfect spiritual makeover as Christ's bride. Through our Anointed One's saving love, you belong to Him for all eternity.

Prayer: Dear Jesus, We kneel at Your throne to worship You as our eternal King. You are true goodness and righteousness. Thank You for claiming us as Your beloved ones, making us over spiritually, and cleansing our hearts in our Baptism. Help us, Lord, to love and honor You above all others all the days of our lives, and keep us in your continual care as we eagerly await the resurrection of all flesh on the Last Day. In Your holy name we pray. Amen.

Diane

Personal Study Questions:
Psalm 45:6–7

1. Which Scriptures quoted in today's faith narrative helped you more tightly connect Jesus' ministry to Psalm 45? How did they do that?

2. What specific words in the psalm verses point to the Messiah's divinity? to His justice and holiness?

3. What (or Who) is the "oil of gladness" in verse 7? (See Acts 10:38.)

4. So what? What does all this mean for you as God's child?

Diane

Psalm 45:8–12

Hear, O daughter, and consider, and incline your ear: forget your people and your father's house, and the king will desire your beauty. Since He is your lord, bow to Him.

A New Allegiance

My father is a pacer. While waiting for something to begin, he has a difficult time sitting still. So he paces, up and down, back and forth. Much of his pacing is due to nervous energy that builds up inside of him because he is one of those people who is nearly always ready to leave earlier than necessary and who, consequently, nearly always arrives much earlier than he needs to. It's become somewhat of a gentle joke around my family that if my dad says he will arrive at 1 p.m., you better be ready for him before noon.

Diane

At no time was my father's pacing more evident to me than on my wedding day. Handsome in his tuxedo hours before the 3:00 p.m. ceremony, he spent the time before we left for the church pacing the blocks near his home. Despite the fact that he could have been inside waiting in air-conditioned comfort, he chose instead to walk around and around the block in 95-degree heat. I noticed him outside pacing back and forth and alerted my mom to his actions. She just smiled at me and said, "Leave your father alone. It's what he needs to do right now."

Not willing to let it go, I marched outside in my wedding gown and veil as I saw him circling the sidewalk for the umpteenth time. I approached my dad and called out, "Hey, Dad, what are you doing? Come on inside and cool off." At my words, my dad turned my way. As he did so, I noticed tears in his eyes, yet he was smiling. Without speaking, he waved me off and kept on walking.

My father's actions mystified me. I couldn't understand why he didn't come in and relax. I couldn't understand why he was crying. After all, for years he had joked about how he couldn't wait to get rid of me! Well, here was his big chance at last. I also was certain that he loved my soon-to-be husband. So what was the deal? And what about that smile? It looked so out of place with his tears. What on earth was going on with my dad?

In Psalm 45:10, God commands a bride, "Forget your people and your father's house." God's Word says that in marriage a man and woman leave their parents and join together to form a new, more important allegiance (Genesis 2:24). As they make their wedding vows, they promise to love, honor, and keep one another, to forsake all others, and to remain united to only each other (Ephesians 5:29–31).

My dad shed a few tears because he knew his family was changing. Once upon a time, my dad knew he was the most important man in my life. He knew I depended on him for care and guidance. My dad was the one who snuck me a little ice cream before I went to sleep. He was the one who taught me how to ride a bike, who took me to the science museum and to the movies. Now, his only daughter was about to be pledged to a man for the rest of her life in a bond that takes precedence over all others. Yes, indeed. My dad knew that because of the new allegiance I would make in just a few short hours, things would be forever different in his family.

But what about the smile? Psalm 45:8, 9, and 12 tell of the beauty of the life a husband and wife can have together, especially as they are made one in Christ. In the allegiance of marriage, a man and woman form a partnership. They pledge to take care of each other in both good and bad times. God designed marriage so children could be created and families could grow (Genesis 1:28). Adorned with fragrance and finery, accompanied by joyful music, the man and woman pledge each other their faithfulness, loyalty, and love.

Even people and nations who do not know Jesus as their Lord and Savior are drawn to Him as they see the happiness we have in Him. As we daily celebrate the love of our Lord in our lives, He gives us the power to show and share His love with those in need of His truth.

No wonder my dad was smiling through his tears! My dad realized that because of marriage, although things would be different, they would be *better*. Better because the new allegiance his daughter was about to make would give him a new golfing partner. Better because in the new allegiance he would gain a son-in-law. Better because someday he might just become a grandpa. And especially better because his daughter was about to gain someone else who would also love and cherish her.

In His Word, God uses the institution of marriage to describe the relationship that all believers have with Jesus. Jesus is our Bridegroom, we are His bride. United in Him, we are His Church. Our Lord comes to claim us dressed in beautiful, fragrant robes (v. 8) that only a true King could wear. His "ivory palaces" represent truth and purity as He Himself is pure and perfect, without sin.

As Christ's bride, we are adorned in "gold of Ophir" (v. 9). This same precious gold once treasured by Solomon (1 Kings 9:28) represents all the gifts our Bridegroom presents us as we are joined by faith to Him. And what wedding gifts Jesus gives us! "But with You there is *forgiveness*" (Psalm 130:4). "Whoever

Diane

believes in the Son has *eternal life*" (John 3:36). "I have said these things to you, that in Me you may have *peace*" (John 16:33). "Greater *love* has no one than this, that someone lay down his life for His friends. You are My friends" (John 15:13–14; emphasis added throughout paragraph).

These wedding gifts from Jesus, our Bridegroom, are all the more precious when you think about who we were without Christ. We were once people without a purpose, separated from God, spiritually dead in our sins. Even in this condition, Jesus loved us. Jesus' love for us is so great that He willingly gave His life and came alive again so He could make us His bride, His Church. All believers in Christ "are no longer strangers and aliens, but you are fellow citizens with the saints and members of the household of God, built on the foundation of the apostles and prophets, Christ Jesus Himself being the cornerstone, in whom the whole structure, being joined together, grows into a holy temple in the Lord" (Ephesians 2:19–22). Because of the relationship Jesus has established through faith with us, we are beautiful to Him (v. 11). Jesus makes our lives infinitely better!

The joy we experience in the new allegiance Jesus creates with us is contagious. Even people and nations who do not know Jesus as their Lord and Savior (v. 12) are drawn to Him as they see the happiness we have in Him. As we daily celebrate the love of our Lord in our lives, He gives us the power to show and share His love with those in need of His truth. By the power of the Holy Spirit, His Church grows and grows, all around the world. It is our King's desire that we all belong to Him (1 Timothy 2:4). He wants everyone to know and believe that He is the one and only way to eternal happiness (John 14:6). He wants everyone to join Him at His heavenly wedding feast.

"Hear, O daughter, and consider, and incline your ear" (v. 10). Jesus loves you. Rejoice that you are joined to Him through faith forever and ever. What a reason we have to smile!

Diane

133

Prayer: Dear Jesus, You are our heavenly Bridegroom. You have claimed all believers as Your Bride, the Church. As You join us together in You, You graciously bless us with Your marvelous gifts of faith, forgiveness, eternal life, peace, and a home with You in heaven. We thank You for all You are and for all You do. Help us to incline our ears and listen always to the truth of Your Word. Help us to grow to love You more and more every day of our lives. Help us to rejoice in Your presence and to show the joy we have in You to others. We praise You, O King, forever and ever. In Your name we pray. Amen.

Diane

thursday

Personal Study Questions: Psalm 45:8–12

1. In what ways do these verses from Psalm 45 help you picture the wedding supper of the Lamb (Revelation 21:9–27)?

2. To what "beauty" might Psalm 45:11 point? From where do we get this beauty despite our sins?

3. Put yourself into the picture painted by verses 8–12. You will one day participate! To what do you most look forward?

4. Consider the comments and Scripture quotations in today's faith narrative concerning the Holy Christian Church. How do they help you see your brothers and sisters in the faith in a different, more positive light?

Diane

Psalm 45:13–17

*I will cause Your name to be remembered
in all generations; therefore nations will
praise You forever and ever.*

Here Comes
the Groom

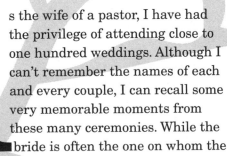

As the wife of a pastor, I have had the privilege of attending close to one hundred weddings. Although I can't remember the names of each and every couple, I can recall some very memorable moments from these many ceremonies. While the bride is often the one on whom the most attention is focused, one of my most vivid wedding memories involves not the bride but the groom.

Diane

It is quite possible that the young man I recall might qualify as the most nervous groom in all of wedding history. His nervousness was quite noticeable from the moment he entered my husband's office at church about an hour prior to the start of the festivities. Although the temperature that day was quite cool, the poor guy was sweating profusely. Despite being dressed in a freshly pressed tuxedo, the groom looked disheveled. His hair was sticking up in all directions from his forehead, perhaps due to an overzealous mousse-and-styling job.

As the clock ticked the minutes until the ceremony, the groom became more and more panicked. My husband calmly talked to him, reassuring him of the various facts they had discussed during the premarital counseling sessions and at the wedding rehearsal the evening before. These words of wisdom seemed to calm him down. But then the ceremony began.

At his appointed time, the overly nervous groom slowly shuffled toward his place in the chancel where he was to stand as he waited for his bride to arrive at the altar. His groomsmen stood close by him, providing much-needed support. So far, so good. But once his bride arrived and as her father gave her over to him, there was a sudden sign of trouble. He began to sway back and forth, looking as if he was about to faint. The bride moved into action, firmly grasping her intended's hand as she led him up the two steps to stand in front of my husband near the altar.

Just as it appeared the crisis was averted and as the ceremony continued as practiced, the groom again began to sway, back and forth, knees locked, ready to collapse. My husband stopped speaking and whispered something to the groom, while his best man came close behind him, ready to catch him should he fall. Those gathered in the sanctuary to witness the wedding began to look at one another, some suppressing nervous giggles at the groom's actions, others obviously concerned for his welfare. Suddenly, the center of attention of the ceremony became not the joining together of two people in Christ or, at the very least, "here comes the bride," but instead, "there goes the groom." It was a sad distraction from what should have been a meaningful wedding

Diane

137

ceremony.

The teetering of the groom continued throughout the ceremony, with brief pauses for reassurance and bracing, until at last, the couple was officially married. As they turned to face the congregation, the groom broke into a relieved smile. He wiped his sweat-soaked brow. The gathered crowd loudly applauded as my husband, also relieved, was finally able to present, "Mr. and Mrs. . . . "

Despite our nationality, our upbringing, our ancestors, even despite our sinful natures, we are all wanted by Jesus. Through God-given faith in His death and resurrection, all who believe in Jesus as the true Savior are united in Him and with Him as His precious people.

The final verses of Psalm 45 paint a picture of a Bridegroom who is quite different from the one I just described. At this wedding ceremony, instead of the groom being a distraction, the Groom is the *attraction*. And rightly so, for verses 13–17 joyfully announce, "Here comes the Groom," your Bridegroom, Jesus!

At this most royal wedding, Jesus' bride, the Church, is led to her King "with joy and gladness" (v. 15). Everyone at this wedding knows they are coming into the presence of the almighty, conquering Savior. As His believers enter His palace, Jesus, our King, majestically stands, full of glory. No one is nervous, especially not the heavenly Bridegroom. This is the moment for which He has waited. The eyes of all nations are on Him. The hearts of all are bursting with joy and love for Jesus alone.

Even many Gentiles, originally part of a group outside of God's kingdom, are there, included as Jesus' sons and daughters (v. 16). As Peter preached in Caesarea, " 'Truly I understand that God shows no partiality, but in every nation anyone who fears Him and does what is right is acceptable to Him. . . . To Him all the prophets bear witness that everyone who believes in Him receives forgiveness of sins through His name' " (Acts 10:34–35, 43). How marvelous! People from all nations are there to worship and honor Jesus. Despite our nationality, our upbringing, our ancestors, even despite our sinful natures, we are all wanted by Jesus. Through God-given faith in His death and resurrection, all who

Diane

believe in Jesus as the true Savior are united in Him and with Him as His precious people.

By the power and desire of God the Father, these believers, filled with the Holy Spirit, share the truth of Jesus "in all generations; therefore nations will praise You forever and ever" (v. 17). Like a new bride gushing over her husband, we gush to those around us about the love and forgiveness we have in Jesus, our Bridegroom. As believer after believer is added to Christ's Church, His faithful continue to praise Him for all He does to make us one in Him. Jesus, our heavenly Groom deserves to be the center of attention, now and forever, for all the right reasons.

" 'I am the Alpha and the Omega,' says the Lord God, 'who is and who was and who is to come, the Almighty' " (Revelation 1:8). Jesus "is coming with the clouds, and every eye will see Him" (Revelation 1:7). And as the angels told the apostles at Jesus' ascension, "This Jesus, who was taken up from you into heaven, will come in the same way as you saw Him go into heaven" (Acts 1:11). When Jesus comes for His bride, the Church, on the Last Day, we will see a Groom who is in total control. The good news is that while right now we have the joy of being a part of Christ's Church as His believers, on that day, He will usher in indescribable joy as He welcomes us into heaven to participate forever and ever at His eternal wedding banquet.

What an exciting promise! But you may wonder, when is our heavenly Bridegroom coming back? Jesus Himself tells us, "Therefore, you also must be ready, for the Son of Man is coming at an hour you do not expect" (Matthew 24:44). For the members of Christ's Church, these words are not a scary warning, for we know that by faith in Jesus we are saved. We are ready. Instead, Jesus' words cause happy anticipation in us. I, for one, can't wait to say with great excitement, "Here comes *the Groom*!" I hope and pray that your hearts, too, are filled with excited yearning for His return as you continue to praise Him forever.

Diane

Prayer: Dearest Lord Jesus, You have claimed us as Your bride! You have placed faith in You in our hearts so we might believe and trust in You as our heavenly Bridegroom, our Lord and Savior. Forever we praise You for Your mighty actions on our behalf in Your death and resurrection and in Your daily care and love for us. Help us to share Your name in all corners of the earth. Keep our hearts filled with joy as we praise You. Keep us alert and watchful in eager anticipation of the day You will return to take us to heaven to Your eternal wedding feast. Come, Lord Jesus, come. In Your glorious name we pray. **Amen.**

Diane

Friday

Personal Study Questions: Psalm 45:13–17

1. The wedding pictured in verses 8–12 dissolves into the eternal marriage of verses 13–17.

   a. In what ways is this picture true—not just in the future, but even now?

   b. In what ways do these words describe the glory that yet awaits us?

2. Why do you suppose Scripture often uses word pictures drawn from marriage to help us understand God's plan for our salvation?

3. Whatever your state in life—single, married, divorced, widowed, engaged—what insights does it give in light of Psalm 45?

Diane

Group Bible Study for Week 4
Psalm 45

1. The faith narratives for this week all quoted many Scriptures, many connecting Jesus, our Savior, with Psalm 45.

   a. Which of these helped you better grasp the full meaning of the psalm?

   b. How did they help you better understand the messianic accents of the psalm?

2. The psalm's title ("superscription") labels it as "a love song" written by the sons of Korah, worship leaders who belonged to Israel's tribe of Levi. Priests and temple workers were drawn from this tribe. While scholars do not consider psalm titles divinely inspired or inerrant, in most cases, they seem logical and fitting.

   a. In what ways does Psalm 45 strike you as a love song?

   b. Who sings it? To whom is it sung?

   c. How does the love song idea enrich your picture of what the corporate worship of God's people today should or could be?

   d. If we sing this song of love to Jesus, what does He sing to us? (See Zephaniah 3:16–17.)

3. Psalm 45:3–5 strikes a chord many would see as romantic. The faith narrative based on these verses invited readers to call to mind knights in shining armor and damsels in distress.

   a. In what ways is Jesus' rescue of us that kind of swoop–and-rescue adventure?

   b. In what ways is it much more earthy—filled with agony, danger, blood, and death? (See Philippians 2:5–10.)

c. How does remembering both the romantic and the earthy deepen the meaning of Psalm 45:3–5 for you?

4. The first half of the psalm describes the Messiah's rescue of His bride. The second half describes their engagement and wedding (vv. 6–12) and marriage (vv. 13–17).

    a. What do you learn from these verses about the Bridegroom, Zion's King?

    b. What do you learn about the bride, Zion, the Holy Christian Church?

    c. What do you learn about yourself, a member of that Church?

    d. How might all this impact your worship?

5. In what ways does Psalm 45:17 evoke the promise of Psalm 2:8? How do both verses encourage you as the daughter of the King, the bride of Christ, to share your Lord's love, beauty, joy, and majesty with those who do not know Him?

6. A child's prayer addresses "tender Jesus, meek and mild."

    a. In what ways have this week's insights from Psalm 45 shown that description of our Lord to be accurate?

    b. In what ways might you now see the description as inadequate or incomplete?

    c. What words from your favorite hymns or prayers might you propose as describing more accurately your Savior from sin, Satan, hell, and death?

7. As a result of this week's study and meditation, how will your relationship with your Bridegroom be different, deeper, and more delightful?

Week Five

Psalm 72

[1] Give the king Your justice, O God,
and Your righteousness to the royal son!
[2] May He judge Your people with righteousness,
and Your poor with justice!
[3] Let the mountains bear prosperity for the people,
and the hills, in righteousness!
[4] May He defend the cause of the poor of the people,
give deliverance to the children of the needy,
and crush the oppressor!

[5] May they fear You while the sun endures,
and as long as the moon, throughout all generations!
[6] May He be like rain that falls on the mown grass,
like showers that water the earth!
[7] In His days may the righteous flourish,
and peace abound, till the moon be no more!

[8] May He have dominion from sea to sea,
and from the River to the ends of the earth!
[9] May desert tribes bow down before Him,
and His enemies lick the dust!
[10] May the kings of Tarshish and of the coastlands
render Him tribute;
may the kings of Sheba and Seba
bring gifts!
[11] May all kings fall down before Him,
all nations serve Him!

¹² For He delivers the needy when He calls,
the poor and him who has no helper.
¹³ He has pity on the weak and the needy,
and saves the lives of the needy.
¹⁴ From oppression and violence He redeems their life,
and precious is their blood in His sight.

¹⁵ Long may He live;
may gold of Sheba be given to Him!
May prayer be made for Him continually,
and blessings invoked for Him all the day!
¹⁶ May there be abundance of grain in the land;
on the tops of the mountains may it wave;
may its fruit be like Lebanon;
and may people blossom in the cities
like the grass of the field!
¹⁷ May His name endure forever,
His fame continue as long as the sun!
May people be blessed in Him,
all nations call Him blessed!

¹⁸ Blessed be the LORD, the God of Israel,
who alone does wondrous things.
¹⁹ Blessed be His glorious name forever;
may the whole earth be filled with His glory!
Amen and Amen!

²⁰ The prayers of David, the son of Jesse, are ended.

Rebekah Curtis

Psalm 72:1–7

*Give the king Your justice, O God, and Your righ-
teousness to the royal son! May He judge Your people
with righteousness, and Your poor with justice!*

Life Isn't Fair

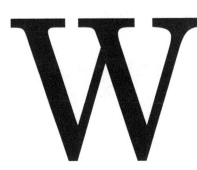 hen my mom asked what I remember her saying most when I was growing up, I didn't even have to think about it: "Life isn't fair!" Whenever I registered an objection to some perceived injustice, this was her ex-

planation. The other kindergarten class gets snacks, but yours doesn't? Life isn't fair. Your friends wear new clothes with brand names, and you wear discount store hand-me-downs? Life isn't fair. You sit on the bench because the girls whose parents fork out the cash for them to play club teams all year are better? Life isn't fair. You didn't get any local scholarships because the kids who were friends with the guidance counselors walked away with all of them? Life isn't fair.

My judicious mom was kind to let me notice for myself, after years of complaining, that I've spent most of my life on the other side of that unfairness. I graduated from college debt-free because those tightwad parents who wouldn't buy me Pantene or Birkenstocks paid my tuition. I financed my grad school whim because I knew a guy who knew a guy who would give me a job. I have a house swarming with laughing, crumb-covered blessings while friends of mine plead with God for just one. Why? Well, life isn't fair.

The unfairness gets uglier. In high school, I traveled with my church's youth group to Haiti for two weeks. We vowed we would never forget the awful poverty we saw there: the malnourished children, the shacks where families of ten or fourteen or seventeen lived, the hospital wards full of feverish invalids tortured by infection, the nameless infants lying alone in orphanage beds, our Haitian friends who wore the same clothes every day. Within a week of returning home, we were throwing away cheeseburgers because they tasted funny, buying new jeans to replace our totally lame old ones, and debating whether the youth center needed Ping-Pong and foosball tables or a new sound system. And, oh yes, telling people how our trip had changed us so much. We would never—*ever!*—be the same after seeing all that.

I hope my friends and I, at least to some extent, grew out of our shortsightedness and learned in the long run to live with more authentic and less rhetorical consideration for our needy brothers and sisters. But no matter what side of life's unfairness you happen to be on at any moment, the fact remains that you can't really do much about it. I could get rid of my closet full of

Rebekah

clothes, move my family to a shack, and send a check for the difference to Haiti, but it wouldn't begin to end the misery there. The gifts God, in His wisdom, has seen fit to give us may be shared but usually can't be transferred. And the crosses He has appointed for us to bear may be lightened by those who love us, but no one can carry them for us entirely.

I sent Grandma silly things in the mail, but I couldn't take the loneliness from her. I put in good words for my friends, but I couldn't give them a pay raise. I sang to my little girl as the nurses held her down, but I couldn't suffer the pain and fear in her place. I had dinner ready and a smile on my face when my husband got home, but I couldn't fix the problems that twisted his demeanor with sadness.

The tragedy is that in our sin-bent world, unfairness is a rational explanation. No matter the size of our case— from a stolen toy to a debilitating disease— the only judge who can put it right is Jesus.

And, on the other side again, my husband got home as early as he could every day, but he couldn't relieve the ache left in my arms by our constantly screaming newborn. My little girl gave me her precious stuffed kitty, but it didn't take away my worries so I could rest. My friends empathized with my predicament, but they couldn't do anything about the choleric landlord skulking outside my walls. My grandma found every folk remedy in the world that my doctor didn't know about, but only more time and pain could heal my wound.

Why did these things happen to me? Why couldn't I do anything for the people I care for so much? Why are people starving in the world, and why can't the people who have enough make it right? I know, Mom—life isn't fair. But there was one thing that my grandma and my little girl and my husband and my friends and I could do: take our case to the One who judges rightly. "Give the king your judgments, O God! Vindicate the afflicted! Save the children of the needy! Crush the oppressor!" These prayers aren't relics of an ancient, politically isolated event. They live right next to the "That's not fair!" festering in the heart of every person. They acknowledge that there is a King who is truly just and who can and will judge fairly. This is the only effective recourse and

Rebekah

comfort we have against the awful unfairness imposed on human existence by our sin.

The King's judgment is terrifying when I'm honest enough to put my sin on the scale. Only He knows better than I how guilty I am of making life unfair. But who's the King here anyway? Am I, or is it the One who put His name on me and welcomed me into His kingdom in Baptism? Are my slanderous and spiteful words stronger than His word of absolution? Can my blighted body stand up to His holy body and precious blood, given and shed for me for the remission of my sins? The answer is on the cross; here is the righteous for the unrighteous to bring me to God: Jesus Christ, King of the Jews and the Gentiles too. The injustice I've deplored, suffered, and even perpetrated is no match for the righteousness of the King, who judges me according to His merits rather than my own. Life as I know it isn't fair—but what I see on Calvary tells me that this isn't real life.

My favorite mom quote came up again lately in a new yet familiar setting. My husband returned from a convention with penlights from some vendor's booth for our two older children, having determined that this was not a baby-safe toy for their one-year-old sister. Little sister was not interested in local safety regulations and at her first opportunity seized a light that had been abandoned. Seeing then that there was another to be had, she took the second light out of her brother's hand and settled into a corner to enjoy, in addition to her plunder, the irony that the kid who wasn't supposed to have even one of the treasures now had them both. The protest began, and I was about to intervene when, to my surprise, my four-year-old closed the conflict by declaring for the benefit of the theft victim, "Well, life isn't fair!" I had to laugh at her flawless usage, not to mention my own inevitable morphing into my mother.

But it also made me sad because there's another thing that isn't fair: children who can't yet read have already learned this lesson to be true. How often does a rational explanation convince a preschooler to stop whining? The tragedy is that in our sin-bent world, unfairness *is* a rational explanation. No matter the size

Rebekah

of our case—from a stolen toy to a debilitating disease—the only judge who can put it right is Jesus. He won the straightening of every crooked place, arthritic hand, and perverse heart by suffering the greatest injustice creation has ever known. Because of His atoning death for us on the cross, we pray for the Father to hasten that day when we and all things will be made eternally right.

Prayer: Lord Jesus, I believe that You will come to be my Judge. Have mercy on me and judge me according to Your compassion. Bring peace to Your people, and let the righteous flourish in Your eternal kingdom. **Amen.**

Rebekah

monday

Personal Study Questions: Psalm 72:1–7

1. In today's faith narrative, the author shares some of her experiences with life's unfairness. How do these echo your own?

2. In what way(s) do the first seven verses of Psalm 72 form a fitting prayer for any person who exercises earthly authority, presiding over the administration of justice?

3. The psalmist, probably King Solomon, asks for several blessings in addition to justice.

   a. Name some of them.

   b. For which of these blessings will you pray today as you take the needs of those in civic authority over you (judges, legislators, governor, president, and others) to the throne of King Jesus?

4. Like the other psalms in this volume of A New Song, Psalm 72 is messianic. It focuses on the Savior God promised to send. What clues in verses 1–7 indicate this?

Rebekah

Psalm 72:8–11

May He have dominion from sea to sea, and from the River to the ends of the earth! May desert tribes bow down before Him, and His enemies lick the dust! May the kings of Tarshish and of the coastlands render Him tribute; may the kings of Sheba and Seba bring gifts! May all kings fall down before Him, all nations serve Him!

Meta-Epiphany

Christmas is busy for everyone. But at my house, Christmas has nothing on Epiphany. I have the privilege of attending a church that hasn't let this holy day fall by the wayside, which means that our gladness doesn't end until the true twelfth day of Christmas. I also have the privilege of seeing that all the trimmings get trimmed for those additional twelve days. Last year, the trouble started on the day when, . . . come to think of it, I never did get those nine ladies dancing. . . .

Rebekah

3 January, 9:30 p.m. My sister contacts me to say she thinks the trumpet part I've given her for the Epiphany service isn't right. I assure her that the computer would have corrected the meter if it were off. She demurs. I bring out my trusty euphonium and offer an online demonstration. The slight delay of Internet communication does not help my case. She grudgingly agrees to continue practicing the part as is, but her doubt remains evident. I note that my throat is a bit scratchy.

4 January, 10:55 a.m. My mother-in-law's plane arrives. On the drive home, we stop by the store to pick up prizes for the winners of the King Cake contest, and I am grateful for Grandma's help getting three children through the parking lot in the cold rain. My two-year-old insists on using the fragrant public bathroom and does a fair job of heeding my command that he not touch *anything*. I also purchase a box of tissues.

5 January, 4:26 a.m. My eight-month-old forcefully requests my company at our regular prebreakfast conference. As I stagger down the hallway, I wonder if I might be *quite sick*.

5 January, 8:30 a.m. Grandma gives me one of the cold-prevention tablets without which she refuses to board a plane. Consuming the tablet is more exciting than I expected. I mention this to Grandma, who informs me that I was supposed to have dissolved it in water first. Grandma keeps the babies out of my way while I spend quality time with the floor and my new box of tissues.

5 January, 10:45 p.m. The first King Cake emerges from the oven. I have not repeated the burning mistake of two years ago, nor will I repeat the cat mistake of last year. I cover my beautiful specimen to protect it from the dessert-loving beast before wobbling upstairs to bed.

6 January, 8 a.m. Construction begins on Cake 2. I bring a chair into the kitchen and work the butter into the gooey dough with the bowl on my lap, breathing over my shoulder and taking frequent breaks to attend to my raw nose and germy hands. I consider making only two cakes but, remembering how close we came to running out last year, resolve to make the third as planned.

Rebekah

153

6 January, noon. The phone rings. It is a lady from church. She says her King Cake isn't rising. I respond with my usual poise: "Huh?" Last year, she says, Pastor told her whoever found the baby had to bring the King Cake next year, so she is making one, but she hasn't used yeast before and doesn't know what to do now that it isn't rising. I am not sure whether to throw my half-kneaded wad of Cake 3 at the wall or credit divine providence for my decision to go ahead with it, considering my friend's cake's rising problems. Note to self: tell husband that his jokes are very funny and confusing.

And we, with the Wise Men, worship the God-man. We bow with all kings at His altar, where we see the real miracle for us this Epiphany: the King of kings, who became a helpless baby so He could die for us and who comes to us now in His body and blood for the forgiveness of our sins.

6 January, 1:30 p.m. Someone knocks on the door. Not Magi. No gifts. They are the visiting pastors who will be assisting with the service. They are here early. Very early! I send them over to the church office to talk shop with my husband. As they walk over, I call my husband and ask if I will need to add feeding his friends to my to-do list. Perhaps I do so rather crankily. He says he is sure they will keep the fast before Holy Communion, as is his custom, and I need not worry.

6 January, 3:00 p.m. The pastors are back. My husband invites them to sit in another room, then quietly asks as I take Cake 3 out of the oven if it is at all possible that they be fed something before church. My wonderful mother-in-law sees my face and tells her wonderful son that she will take care of it.

6 January, 3:30 p.m. My sister arrives with her trumpet. We bust out the brass and have a decent practice, considering the difficulty I have with filling my lungs. The part we negotiated three days ago is . . . okay. We're sure it will work out at game time.

6 January, 4 p.m. I invite the babies into the kitchen, from which they have been banned for the last twelve hours, to assist me in icing the King Cakes. My just-turned-four-year-old reminds me just in time to hide the baby inside. Cakes 1 and 2 look great, or as great as King Cakes ever look. (Purple, yellow, and green?

Rebekah

Who thought of this color scheme?) Clever four-year-old reminds me to hide the baby in Cake 3, just in time. I become maudlin over the prospect of my sad, sick self hauling the sticky lumps across the tundra to the parish hall. Then I remember the pastor menagerie in the next room. They gamely trudge through the frosty grass, one cake each.

6 January, 5:30 p.m. Grandma has somehow conjured, from the dubious contents of my refrigerator, supper for everyone in the house. I marvel at the serendipity of her visit falling on this particular day. The only person I have to feed is the baby.

6 January, 7 p.m. Everyone is clean, dressed, and in a pew at the proper time. It only seems like the Epiphany miracle. My cake-bearers have been transformed into deacon, preacher, and celebrant. They are wearing the beautiful white and gold vestments my mother-in-law heroically finished sewing in time for the service. My beleaguered nose discerns the gentle perfume of the air, adorned with frankincense for this celebration. The humble brass section joins the organ to fill our little church with the ringing joy of salvation for the Gentiles, for us.

I position myself behind my euphonium so the baby, sitting with Grandma, won't see me and keep me from playing the postlude. I am tempted to think about how I'm going to get from the church to the parish hall before everybody else. But it's Epiphany, and this is the hour we've all been working so hard to reach— *Lord, let me seek You where You may be found, here in Your Word and Sacrament, where You have promised to be.* "May the kings of Tarshish and of the coastlands render Him tribute; may the kings of Sheba and Seba bring gifts! May all kings fall down before Him, all nations serve Him!" (Psalm 72:10) the choir chants. And we, with the Wise Men, worship the God-man. We bow with all kings at His altar, where we see the real miracle for us this Epiphany: the King of kings, who became a helpless baby so He could die for us and who comes to us now in His body and blood for the forgiveness of our sins.

6 January, 8 p.m. The bright notes of "Jesus Has Come and Brings Pleasure" spring out the door with the faithful, who scurry

Rebekah

across the street to claim their slice of cake and look for the baby. It was good to be here, but we must return to the plain. I pack up my instrument and run down the stairs to beat them there, stopping by the house on the way to pick up the prizes (king-size candy bars, of course). A fourth cake is waiting on the counter, having risen enough after all. A few minutes later, cakes decimated and prizes distributed, Grandma and I lean against the wall with cups of fortifying red Kool-Aid. The young pastor comes over and thanks us for our work. "Sure," we say with tired smiles. But our work wasn't for him, and our gifts were so small compared to what we have been given tonight. The kings of the earth and even we peasants may offer gifts, but our King *is* the gift.

Prayer: Lord Jesus, thank You for grafting me into Your family and counting me among Your children. Let me be worthy of Your name and of the gifts You offer me. Amen.

Rebekah

156

Personal Study Questions:
Psalm 72:8–11

1. From verse 8 onward, it becomes more obvious that Solomon has a bigger topic in mind than his own earthbound administration. What gives you that sense?

2. How do verses 8–11 form a suitable prayer for . . .

   a. the Epiphany celebration of God's people as we recall the gift of the Christ Child and the visit of the Magi?

   b. the Great Commission, missionary, evangelistic work of Christ's Church?

3. For what people-groups and nations do you regularly pray? How is God at work in hearts and lives in those places? How could you learn more about the work there and, thus, begin to pray more specifically?

Rebekah

Psalm 72:12–14

For He delivers the needy when he calls, the poor and him who has no helper. He has pity on the weak and the needy, and saves the lives of the needy. From oppression and violence He redeems their life, and precious is their blood in His sight.

Delivery

Poor Mary, I thought, squirming for a tolerable arrangement of myself in the cushionless pew. My 10-pound beach ball of a belly lounged on my lap as I examined the program to see when I'd have to stand again. A fourth-grade Caesar Augustus had just issued his decree, which heartlessly called for a girl exactly as pregnant as I was, and years younger, to get herself 70 miles from home. Donkey or no, the trip would have been miserable. I wondered if the *Magnificat* had still been running through her head on that journey or perhaps something more along the lines of *De profundis*.

Rebekah

158

When my doctor told me months earlier that my due date was Christmas Day, I groaned. My husband and I were leaving soon for his vicarage assignment. Having grown up in a pastor's family, I knew there could be no worse timing for a baby than a major holiday. "Don't worry," she assured me while showing me the door, "they never come on their due dates. You'll go late when all the busyness is over." Easy for her to say—I'd be hundreds of miles away and safely out of her appointment book by then. Before the paling of the stars on December 25, I vindictively wished I was calling her away from her tree and presents as punishment for that false prophecy! We ran the red light in front of church en route to the hospital just as my husband should have been stepping into the pulpit.

There is no weakness, no neediness, no poverty of strength or spirit like labor. I learned that day, as do all women in childbirth, what it means to have no helper. Neither the crabby doctor (impatient to get back to her heart-healthy tofurkey), nor the soothing nurses (resigned to working on Christmas), nor my labor coach husband (almost as scared as I was, despite our scrupulous prepping) could get that baby out for me. If there had been room for a tune in my panicking brain over the course of those hours, it definitely wouldn't have been the *Magnificat*. Out of the depths did I cry to God for His mercy that day, absolutely helper-less under the curse of my sin.

Both the baby and I ended up delivered, God be praised, and I've determined that it's a rather profitable spiritual exercise to despair of one's life every twentyish month and have kept it up. But the pain, fear, and humiliation of childbirth are only a distillation of human life. No strength for another contraction or another day of mistreatment at the hands of a manipulative boss. No comfort of knowing when the ordeal will end or when the past-curfew teenager will walk in the door. No dignity in lying a mangled mess under bright lights while the doctor sorts sutures or in making excuses for the obvious symptoms of an illness that you're not ready to make public. Sin takes every opportunity to punish us, playing dirty and hitting hard whether we're at the top

Rebekah

159

or the bottom of our game.

Whose life illustrates this more faithfully than the mother of our Lord? Her esteem in the eyes of God cost her reputation before men. She loved as all mothers, but her Son knew He must love His true Father more than He loved her and did not look back longingly into her sad eyes when He put His hand to the task. She understood Him as only a mother can, but He rebuffed her when His understanding repeatedly exceeded hers. She sacrificed the life she could have had for Him only to suffer the nightmare of watching her child die, knowing that He sacrificed Himself in the same obedience to the Father's will that had been hers so many years before. Poor Mary, yet how rich in her poverty! Her cruel sorrows could not overcome the joy that was hers in being the mother of God; her beloved Son broke sin and death to heal her broken heart. The sin my own twisted heart loves so much could not overpower the love of Jesus, who died to redeem my life from sin and its curse.

Her baby died for my baby, my mother's baby, and all the babies of our mother Eve. I marveled that because of Mary's baby, my new scars and memories of pain, still so fresh and horrifying, would someday be gone forever, and that God Himself would wipe every tear from my eyes. And my soul magnified the Lord.

The light shines in the darkness, but the darkness has not understood it. At one point in my delivery I offered a pitiful prayer that the nurse attending me overheard. She nodded encouragingly and pointed to a pin on her scrubs exhorting me in rhinestones: BELIEVE. "That's right, Honey," she said to me. "Just believe." I felt annoyed. I did not need a personal pep talk. I was completely earnest in begging the Creator of the universe for His help, and I believed that He would answer me according to His promise to deliver the needy when they call.

I know the nurse meant to make me feel better, and her intention was very kind. But her words still prickled. There is no such thing as "just" believing. Belief is true or false, holy or demonic. To have my faith in the Savior turned into a platitude, equating the power of the cross with the power of positive think-

Rebekah

ing, angered me at a time when I needed that Savior so desperately. Faith is the *assurance* of things hoped for. Anything less is pure foolishness. If there were no one to hear and rescue me, then my prayer was no prayer, but a feeble-minded delusion veiling an insidious lie. Another contraction spared the considerate nurse from having to hear my thoughts on the subject, while I consoled myself with the knowledge that a little postmodern pseudo-spirituality could not negate the promise of God to hear and help me—which He did.

Late that Christmas night, I pondered all these things in my heart. It had been my worst Christmas ever: I had felt so deeply the awful strength of God's Word against me while His curse mauled and terrified me. Of course, it was also my best Christmas ever as my husband and I, a shameless live-action cliché, grinned like idiots over our squashy treasure. The mother who shared her first-baby-day celebration with me poked into my thoughts again, and my heart ached to know that she had had no soft bed like the one where I was finally resting. Her baby died for my baby, my mother's baby, and all the babies of our mother Eve. I marveled that because of Mary's baby, my new scars and memories of pain, still so fresh and horrifying, would someday be gone forever and that God Himself would wipe every tear from my eyes. And my soul magnified the Lord.

Prayer: Lord Jesus, I am poor and weak, and only You can help me. Have mercy on me and save me for the sake of Your suffering and death. Deliver me out of the trials of this life, and raise me to Your everlasting kingdom in Your good time. Amen.

Rebekah

wednesday

Personal Study Questions:
Psalm 72:12–14

1. In what ways do verses 12–14 describe the actions of a godly, compassionate, just earthly ruler?

2. In the deepest sense, these verses describe our Lord Jesus. How so?

3. When have you felt needy and helpless, as did the author of the psalm and the author of today's faith narrative? How did Jesus help you then?

Psalm 72:15–17

May His name endure forever,
His fame continue as long as the sun! May people
be blessed in Him, all nations call Him blessed!

Children of the Heavenly Father

My living arrangements in high school were a really raw deal. I had my own room furnished with a serviceable bed, a pantry stocked for fallout following a nuclear attack, a vehicle for my use alone, and clothes that not only fit but were also not quite unfashionable enough to jeopardize my social opportunities without assistance from my personality. None of this did I finance; however, the lavish room and board did come with a price: it had to be shared with a ninth grader and two seventh graders. The *outrage*! That a sophisticate like myself should be forced to live alongside these unspeakably annoying children! This was all a terrible hardship to me.

But when I came back for Thanksgiving break my freshman year of college, those annoying kids didn't really bother me that much. Sometimes the twins actually seemed kind of funny. My sister didn't make me feel guilty for the clothes I left all over the place and was as much fun to talk to as my roommate.

I know whom I have to thank for it: Father and mother, God and His Church. His lovingly wrought instruction, her gentle guiding voice, and the forgiveness He delivers through her in the means of grace continue shaping me and all of His children more into the likeness God intended for us to have—His own.

Back at school, I found myself looking forward to seeing my parents *and* that random group of other humans that lived with them. By the time "the little kids" were in college, the only thing that would make us angry with one another was when somebody had a friend over to alloy our unicameral hangouts. When we all had a chance to see what the world was like, we learned how good we had it back with people who, by our standards, knew what was going on. Our unity was a fortress of private jokes, Mom's singular lasagna, an argot bewildering to outsiders, and—most significantly—the faith in which God had graciously preserved all of us.

We all knew we had our parents to thank for it. They put up with our bickering and complaining and kept giving us what we needed, although we didn't know we needed it and certainly never thanked them sufficiently for it. Their love was so much bigger than our petty selfishness that with lots of patience and perseverance, they transformed a barbarian horde into a group of moderately responsible civilians.

The same thing happens in our churches. By the grace of God, new members are born into His family through the saving waters of Baptism. Next thing you know, those new members are screaming so loudly during sermons that they have to be hauled out by their embarrassed mothers. They can't remember the Third Article of the Creed on their catechism quizzes. They monopolize Bible class time with irrelevant questions. They get into ridiculous fights with brothers and sisters in Christ. They give offerings

Rebekah

164

grudgingly and wish they could sleep in on Sunday mornings. They are mysteriously never around to answer the phone during the week when the VBS committee calls for volunteers. By "they," of course, I mean "I." It's no secret to my church family that I have a lot of spiritual growing up to do.

Just like that Thanksgiving break when I found home had changed—or something like that—as life goes on, I learn more and more that God, my Father, and my mother, the Church, know what I need much better than I do. For a long time, I harbored a belligerent chip on my shoulder about church being pointless and boring. When I finally bothered to listen to one of the many people who sought caringly to correct my understanding of what church was for, I became truly glad to go the house of the Lord to receive His gift of forgiveness. My impious heart conspires with my lazy flesh to keep me in bed for another half hour every single morning, but I've never regretted shaking off that dull sloth to accept God's invitation to prayer. The words and promises of God had been declaring to me all along that these were the right things to do, and the teachings of the Church were there quietly urging me to take my Lord at His Word. Why didn't, and don't, we just do what we're told in the first place? We're very authentic *children* of God, which is to say, shortsighted, self-centered, immature, and disobedient. We would be utterly lost without His longsuffering love for us.

God shows His love for us in this: while we were still sinners, Christ died for us. My parents never let my diapers and back-talking and slovenliness and ingratitude excuse them from their commitment to me. Jesus didn't let my hate for Him and love for every sin keep Him from going to the cross for me. I learn to love the family of God as I learned to love the family into which I was born. It starts with a cold jolt and involves plenty of pain, anger, humiliation, frustration, and people I don't want to like, but I've sure changed a lot along the way. I learned that the sister in Christ who was so bothersome at Bible study was a much closer ally than the friendly girl whose locker next to mine was wallpapered with pro-abortion slogans. I can even acknowledge

Rebekah

165

that helping with VBS has its gratifying moments. I know whom I have to thank for it: Father and mother, God and His Church. His lovingly wrought instruction, her gentle guiding voice, and the forgiveness He delivers through her in the means of grace continue shaping me and all of His children more into the likeness God intended for us to have—His own.

I still have my disagreements with my brothers and sisters in Christ; it's hard for us to coexist among all our differences, and we often don't agree with or even understand one another. But we have all been baptized into the one name that endures forever. We have all been fed with the abundant bread of life, and our thirst has been quenched with the same fruit of the vine. Each of us has been blessed with forgiveness by the King who rules us and adopts us into the most wonderful, mixed-up family in all creation. We bless the name of Jesus, which binds us to Himself and each other, and look forward to the day when He will grow us out of all our childish selfishness and make us to blossom together in the eternal city of God.

Prayer: Lord Jesus, forgive me for my rebellious and ungrateful heart, and teach me to be thankful for the abundant blessings You have given me. Become greater in me every day, and make me a blessing to my brothers and sisters who share Your eternal name. Amen.

Rebekah

Personal Study Questions:
Psalm 72:15–17

1. What hints to do you see in these verses that the Messiah is . . .

   a. eternal (without beginning or end)?

   b. merciful and gracious toward His people?

   c. worthy of praise?

2. How does Jesus fully and ultimately fit these characteristics?

3. What blessings do you, like the author of today's faith narrative, find in belonging to His people, His Holy Christian Church?

Rebekah

Psalm 72:18–20

*Blessed be the L*ORD*, the God of Israel, who alone does wondrous things. Blessed be His glorious name forever; may the whole earth be filled with His glory! Amen and Amen! The prayers of David, the son of Jesse, are ended.*

With All the Company of Heaven

A few weeks after my grandma died, an angel asked the disciples, "Why do you stand looking into heaven?" I was in church on Ascension, and I knew how the men on the mountain felt. The person they loved was gone, and what were they supposed to do? There they stood with their

Rebekah

heads back and mouths open, not knowing how to get on with things. Grandma had never lived more than a few blocks from us. Now there was no one on the other side of her door to loan me a needle or watch *Wheel of Fortune* with, and I couldn't get my mind around it. Maybe if I just stood in the doorway between our house and her apartment, like the disciples looking at the sky, I wouldn't have to figure out the new protocols for life without her.

The world offers a broad and easy comfort to the bereaved. "Grandma is looking down on you and smiling," it says. "Grandma is right there next to you, proud of you and helping you in everything you do." Well, I knew that was all nonsense. Grandma was at rest with Jesus, not hovering around the room smiling invisibly—and it's a good thing, considering how often I'm doing things I wouldn't want her looking in on. The pastor conducted her small family funeral without any delusional fairy tales about disembodied dead people floating indulgently through our ceiling fans and holding the cobwebs away from us. He allowed us true mourning by proclaiming the truth of our sin, forgiveness, and resurrection in Jesus.

It would be easy to fall for that fairy tale, to imagine Grandma here and happy with me when I want her to be, without having to bother with all that sin and repentance and atonement and forgiveness and mystery. But we do not grieve as those who have no hope. A pastor once told me of a funeral he had conducted at which some family members of the deceased were not Christian. A young man had died, and after the service, his mother wailed like a child and clung to the body so violently that the pastor feared she would pull it out of the casket. At another funeral, an old man's unbelieving son sat and listened stone-faced and disdainful at the proclamation of forgiveness and eternal life in Jesus. Whether driven to carnal howling or cauterized past feeling, the souls of those who do not know our Lord can disclose themselves in unsettling clarity at life's end.

Neither do we grieve as those who swallow the world's false hope. It is common for the "spiritual" among us to dress up death just as they dress up God: with all the mean and sad-making

Rebekah

parts amputated, remade in our toothless image. When death comes along, they take away that nasty black robe and sickle, smear blush onto the hard bones, and force smiles at the monstrosity they've propped up behind the punch bowl. They throw a party instead of a funeral to "celebrate life," quaver out cheery ditties to smother the dirges their souls privately weep, and treacherously suppress the truth: that death is bad and acting as if it isn't makes it infinitely dangerous.

All the saints who have gone before us gather together with us where heaven meets earth at our Lord's altar. They are with Him always, we are with Him there, and to be with Him is to be with them. Communion is no series of private meetings; Jesus and me, Jesus and you, Jesus and them. It is the communion of saints, who cannot be divided into the dead and the living, for in Christ are all made alive.

What can prevent the fragile creatures that we are from becoming panicking lunatics or insensate psychopaths, making us functional even in our anguish? How can the human heart openly face the stark horror of death and not despair? There is no wonder like this: that the greatest human terror can be made into simple, though immense, sadness. Only someone who defeated death, and not only for Himself, but for us, could transform it so dramatically. We who know Jesus know that He has borne our griefs on the cross and carried our sorrows to the grave. His death for us means that even when we walk through the valley of its shadow, we fear no evil. We do not fall for the dangerous foolishness of forcing death to masquerade as a "celebration of life," pretending that our tears are somehow wrong or inferior to the joy we rightly know at other times. Certainly we do not scream in primal fear or sneer in cynical, damning ignorance. We see death for what it is: our final, and defeated, enemy. We mourn, knowing that we are blessed in doing so, for the Lord of life has promised that we will be comforted.

But still we are sad, and sadness is no trifle either. Grandma's belongings seemed so familiar until it was our job to go through the dressers and jewelry boxes and figure out what to do with all of them. We didn't know how to walk past her door without stopping by to say hi to her. Those gaudy caricatures of

Rebekah

170

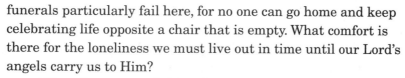

funerals particularly fail here, for no one can go home and keep celebrating life opposite a chair that is empty. What comfort is there for the loneliness we must live out in time until our Lord's angels carry us to Him?

When Jesus ascended into heaven, the disciples were a confused crew. They had thought Jesus was gone once, and that hadn't been true, so how could He be gone again? "This Jesus, who was taken up from you into heaven, will come in the same way as you saw Him go into heaven," explained the angels (Acts 1:11). Wouldn't they—and we—miss Him terribly until then? Yes, but our Jesus, who loves us so much, would not leave us completely alone. "I am with you always, to the end of the age," He promised (Matthew 28:20). And, "This is My body which is for you. . . . This cup is the new covenant in My blood" "which is poured out for many for the forgiveness of sins" (1 Corinthians 11:24–25; Matthew 26:28). He hosts in the flesh the Supper to which He invites us and all the living, so that with angels and archangels and all the company of heaven, we see and worship Him there.

With all the company of heaven. With Grandma, who lives not with me, but with Him. With her husband, my grandpa, from whom she was separated by death years before I was born. All the saints who have gone before us gather together with us where heaven meets earth at our Lord's altar. They are with Him always, we are with Him there, and to be with Him is to be with them. Communion is no series of private meetings—Jesus and me, Jesus and you, Jesus and them. It is the communion of saints, who cannot be divided into the dead and the living, for in Christ are all made alive.

Grandma was buried next to my grandpa in the city where they raised their family, several hours from where any of us now live. I don't know if she ever visited his gravesite in my lifetime, and we rarely visit hers. Our comfort isn't there anyway. Our comfort is in Jesus, who makes His resurrection ours and gives us a real and eternal hope. Our comfort is His glorious presence among us in His holy body and precious blood, given and shed for the remission of our sins. And as if that weren't enough, we also have

Rebekah

the joy of knowing that when we meet Him at His altar in our truest worship, receiving His gifts, we worship also with all the saints. Venerable saints Mary and John, humble saints Jack and Elsie, and even I, the sorriest saint, miraculously gather together in His sanctuary. There we sing "bless the LORD, the God of Israel, who alone does wondrous things" (Psalm 72:18).

Prayer: Lord Jesus, thank You for Your gracious provision of communion with You and all Your saints, which comforts me so wholly through this life's sadnesses. Increase in me Your humility, that I will be fit to see Your glory when You come again to raise me and all the dead. Amen.

Rebekah

Friday

Personal Study Questions: Psalm 72:18–20

1. What "wondrous things" has your Lord Jesus, the King of love, done in your life this week? Praise Him!

2. Note the repeated "Amen" in verse 19. The repetition emphasizes the certainty that "this shall be so." Skim the psalm again. For what promised blessings, certain to come about, are you most thankful?

Rebekah

Group Bible Study for Week 5
Psalm 72

1. Tell about a faith narrative or passage from this week's psalm that struck you as especially meaningful.

2. Skim through the entirety of Psalm 72 to find evidence of it being . . .

    a. a fitting prayer for godly earthly leadership in your town, city, state, and nation.

    b. a prayer concerning the promised Messiah.

3. Several verses in Psalm 72 focus on the "poor," "weak," "oppressed," and "needy" (vv. 4, 12, 13, 14). Sometimes we rush to spiritualize words like this in Scripture, neglecting questions of how we could more faithfully enact our Lord's concern for those who lack adequate food, clothing, housing, basic safety, and other necessities of life.

    a. What might lie behind our tendency to want to ignore our neighbor's physical needs?

    b. Prophets like Amos and apostles like James will not let us get away with this neglect of concern for the needs of others. (See, for example, Amos 4:1–3 and James 5:1–6.) Why not?

    c. Still, sin and Satan are the ultimate oppressors. If not for sinful selfishness and greed, earth would be much more of a paradise, an Eden. Wherever the true Gospel of Jesus has taken root and flourished, the society has become more just, and the poor have been more fairly treated. Where do you see this (or its opposite) happening in your own community? your own church?

    d. What else might Jesus want you to be doing in either your community or your church to care for the poor and oppressed?

4. Read Psalm 72:12–14 again. Would a candidate for public office who ran on a platform like the one described in these verses be electable? Defend your answer.

5. When sin and Satan oppress us, when we are weak and needy, our Lord has compassion on us. In mercy, He sent Jesus to be our helper, our deliverer, our Savior. Because our blood is precious in His sight, Jesus shed His own blood for us. (See vv. 12–14.)

a. God's concern for us and His mercy toward us begins with His forgiveness for all our sins. But His love extends beyond that to His help in every time of need. What examples of this mercy can you cite from your own life or from the lives of other believers that would encourage the members of your group?

b. How does your Lord's mercy toward you in every need encourage you as you face family or job concerns, illness, or any other adversity today?

6. With all this in mind, how do verses 18–19 provide an appropriate chorus of praise in response to God's care? How could your group best incorporate these verses into today's closing prayer?

Week Six

Psalm 98

[1] Oh sing to the LORD a new song,
for He has done marvelous things!
His right hand and His holy arm
have worked salvation for Him.
[2] The LORD has made known His salvation;
He has revealed His righteousness in the sight of the nations.
[3] He has remembered His steadfast love and faithfulness
to the house of Israel.
All the ends of the earth have seen
the salvation of our God.

[4] Make a joyful noise to the LORD, all the earth;
break forth into joyous song and sing praises!
[5] Sing praises to the LORD with the lyre,
with the lyre and the sound of melody!
[6] With trumpets and the sound of the horn
make a joyful noise before the King, the LORD!

[7] Let the sea roar, and all that fills it;
the world and those who dwell in it!
[8] Let the rivers clap their hands;
let the hills sing for joy together
[9] before the LORD, for He comes
to judge the earth.
He will judge the world with righteousness,
and the peoples with equity.

Heather Melcher

Psalm 98:1

Oh Sing to the LORD a new song, for He has done marvelous things! His right hand and His holy arm have worked salvation for Him.

He Has Done Marvelous Things

I have a love-hate relationship with romance stories. Part of me delights in the over-the-top men in movies and television shows. At first, it's fun to imagine what it would be like to have a man fly halfway across the world to declare his love for me or fill my apartment with flowers or risk his life to save me from kidnappers. But when I start comparing my real-world husband to these stories, I wind up feeling neglected and unappreciated.

My husband and I met when I was twenty-seven. I hadn't dated much before meeting him, and I had stored up a sizable inventory of romantic ideas after a childhood of creating dreamy courtships and weddings for my dolls and years of watching romantic movies and television shows. I had high hopes that this new boyfriend would fulfill all of my marvelously idealistic dreams.

Although there were romantic moments while we were dating, I often felt like something was missing. Rather than romantic candlelit dinners, dancing, and bouquets of flowers, we mostly made meals at one of our homes, watched rented videos together, and visited each other at work as our schedules allowed. Once we were married, it seemed that there was even less movie-style romance. We were busy setting up a home together and learning how to live with someone after years of living alone. First we were busy with jobs, then a child, and now another child is on the way. There's rarely enough time for a good night's sleep, much less candlelit dinners or walks on a beach.

Our real-life romance bears little resemblance to the ideals of movies and television, but my husband has his own way of showing his love for me that is far more special than any dinners, dancing, flowers, candy, or jewelry could ever be. He does things that require a sacrifice of his time and energy, which are far more scarce and valuable.

His practical kind of romance started when we were dating. If we were driving two vehicles somewhere, he insisted on driving behind me so he could see if I had any problems and would be able to stop to help me. When the weather turned really cold, he made sure to check the gas door on my car every time we were together because it kept freezing shut.

The practical romance continued after we married and has become even more appreciated since having our first child. Once, when our son was about a year old, he had a horrific poopy diaper blowout that covered our little darling from armpits to ankles and then got smeared on the carpet, sofa, and his toys. My husband happened to call just as I was trying to figure out how to get both him and the room cleaned up. I was close to tears, and once my husband heard what was going on, he dropped his work in the farm shop and came home to help me get the mess under control. At that moment, I wouldn't have traded all the long-stemmed red roses in the world for that half hour my husband gave me.

As I write this, I'm eight months pregnant. I feel huge, tired, and awkward most of the time. Romance for me right now is when my husband takes our three-year-old with him for a while so I can rest. Romance is my husband checking my legs to see if I'm retaining water and, if I am, telling me to go sit with my feet up while he makes dinner. Romance is my husband telling me I'm beautiful and looking like he really means it when I'm cranky, feel as big as a house, and have puffy, black circles under my eyes.

Happiness on earth is useless if we don't have faith and eternal life with God. God's miraculous works are aimed at saving us from our sin (justification) and helping us to grow in faith (sanctification). His goal is for us to be spiritually safe and healthy. Like a romantic leading man, God wants to make us His and keep us His.

My husband does marvelous, selfless things for me because he cares about my well-being. His main goal is for me to be safe and healthy. On those occasions when he does give me flowers or a card or takes me out for a nice dinner, I feel a little guilty that my heart doesn't sing with the same intensity of love and appreciation as it did when he helped clean up that poopy mess.

My Christian husband reflects the kind of love that God has for us. The marvelous things God does for us are not just extravagant shows of affection. Although I'm sure He likes to see us happy, our happiness and comfort are not His main goal. Happiness on earth is useless if we don't have faith and eternal life with God. God's miraculous works are aimed at saving us from our sins (justification) and helping us to grow in faith (sanctification). His goal is for us to be spiritually safe and healthy.

In the Bible, we read that God did marvelous things, such as parting the Red Sea to save His people from the Egyptians and causing the walls of Jericho to fall so His people could take

Heather

possession of the land He had promised them. His plan was to keep a remnant of believers alive and to provide a homeland for them until the time came for His most marvelous gift, when He sent His Son, Jesus, to die for our sins and then raised Him to life again. His gift of love didn't end there. Jesus, our Bridegroom, also went to heaven to prepare a perfect home for us for all eternity, and He sent the Holy Spirit to comfort and guide us until He comes back to take us to heaven. Even the most extravagant movie romance can't compare to the marvelous things God has done for us.

Romance stories often end with the words "and they lived happily ever after." In real life, none of us ever experience happily ever after. Life is full of stresses such as unexpected bills, illness, death, and other problems. Turn to Revelation 21 to read about the only true happily ever after any of us get—when we go to heaven to be with Jesus forever:

And I heard a loud voice from the throne, saying, "Behold, the dwelling place of God is with man. He will dwell with them, and they will be His people, and God Himself will be with them as their God. He will away wipe every tear from their eyes, and death shall be no more, neither shall there be mourning, nor crying, nor pain anymore, for the former things have passed away." (Revelation 21:3–4)

If that's not something marvelous enough to sing about, I don't know what is. Choose your favorite hymn or song of praise, and take the time to sing a love song to God today. Remember that He gave you the voice you have, and no matter what you think it sounds like, it's beautiful to Him. "Sing to the Lord a new song, for He has done marvelous things!" (Psalm 98:1).

Heather

Prayer: I praise You, Lord, for all the marvelous things You have done and continue to do! Please help me to see and appreciate Your love and provision for me in my everyday life. Thank You so much for sending Jesus to save me from my sin and for preparing a dream home for us to be together forever in heaven. Let every song I sing to you be filled with Your love, for Your mercies are new every morning. Alleluia! Amen.

Heather

monday

Personal Study Questions:
Psalm 98:1

1. Today's faith narrative reflects on romantic deeds of kindness the author's husband does for her, like making sure the gas tank is filled during cold weather and helping to clean up a dirty baby.

   a. What everyday blessings from your Lord evoke a "new song" from your heart today?

   b. What truly "marvelous things" in your life also evoke your songs of praise?

2. When we could not work salvation for ourselves, the Lord's "right hand and His holy arm" did it for us! Unpack the word *salvation*. What gifts of God's grace have come to you in His "salvation package"? Thank Him for them.

Heather

Psalm 98:2

The Lord has made known His salvation;
He has revealed His righteousness
in the sight of the nations.

Revealed in His Time

I am a planner. I like to have things figured out and organized well ahead of time. I knew which university I wanted to attend when I was in the fifth grade and began saving tuition money before I even started junior high school. I spent endless hours working out best-case scenarios for career, marriage, and having children. And I probably put as much effort into planning every detail of my wedding as goes

Heather

into organizing the Olympics.

The problem with my planning is that I very rarely come up with the same plan God has for me. I try to seek His will and use Scripture and prayer to guide my goals, but I lack His ability to see the big picture or even all the options. Life regularly shows me that it is really God, and not me, who is in control.

One of my goals as a child and teen was to have at least one Christian friend who was about the same age as me and who would understand my faith. It didn't seem like much to ask. I poured out countless prayers asking for God to give me such a friend, but nothing happened. I tried to develop a plan to locate such a friend on my own. I looked for a Christian friend at Sunday School and youth group. When I didn't find someone who understood me at my own church, I attended another church and its youth group for a while. I went to a Lutheran camp each summer with high hopes that I would find that Christian friend I longed for. But, each year I came home frustrated, discouraged, and lonely. I knew that God always answers prayer. I just wasn't sure if I should accept that He had said "no" or hope He was just saying "wait."

One day, God finally said "yes" to my prayer. It was only a month or two into my first year of university. I had been carpooling from the suburbs with a friend I'd known since second grade. Since I didn't have a car, I'd been paying for gas to share expenses. One morning, after we'd gotten to school, she told me she didn't want to carpool together anymore and I'd need to find another way home that night because she had to leave early. Then she left me sitting in the cafeteria area of the student union building feeling shocked and betrayed. I had already been feeling overwhelmed by the adjustment to university, and this surprise rejection from one of my oldest friends was almost too much to handle.

I was on the verge of tears and was about to head to the bathroom to compose myself before anybody saw me "lose it," when a girl from my high school came to the table where I was sitting. It was Joanna, our former student body prime minister (I grew up in Canada). I'd spoken with her a few times in high

Heather

school, and she'd seemed nice enough, but she was beautiful, popular, smart, and always seemed to be wearing the perfect outfit. I was surprised she even recognized me, and the last thing I felt like doing was pull myself together enough to have a chat.

I braced, expecting to feel uncomfortable and wondering how I could get out of this ordeal politely. But as we started talking, I forgot who I thought she was and felt like everything would be okay. To my surprise, I wound up sharing that I'd lost my ride home. She shared that she'd spilled her coffee and was having a terrible morning too. She lived only a few minutes' drive from my house and offered to give me a ride home. We arranged a time and place to meet at the end of the day and parted to go to our different classes.

I love to see the artistry with which God weaves our lives together to work for our good. The more I read the Bible, the more I see that same artistry in the history of the world. The whole Bible, both Old Testament and New Testament, work together as one story of how God carried out His plan to save us from our sins and reveal that plan of salvation to us.

As the time approached for us to meet, I started getting nervous. Visiting in the cafeteria for a few minutes was one thing, but an hour confined in a car together could get pretty awkward if we ran out of things to say. I started thinking that maybe figuring out the bus schedule wouldn't have been so bad after all. But when we met at the end of the day, things instantly felt comfortable again. We talked the whole way out to the parking lot and all the way home. I kept thinking how surprised I was that nothing she said was contrary to my beliefs and that she never once hurt my feelings. We continued carpooling together, and in the years since God gave me Joanna's friendship, she and I have grown as close as sisters.

This friendship God arranged for me is only one of the many plans I've seen unfold in my life. I love to see the artistry with which God weaves our lives together to work for our good. The more I read the Bible, the more I see that same artistry in the history of the world. The whole Bible, both Old Testament and New Testament, work together as one story of how God carried out His plan to save us from our sins and reveal that plan of salvation to us. God revealed His salvation to the world over and over again

Heather

through miracles such as saving Noah and his family, parting the Red Sea, and, ultimately, through Jesus' death and resurrection. But He also reveals His care for each of us personally through people and circumstances in our lives. God reveals His salvation to us in much the same way that He gave Joanna's friendship to me.

When God decided it was time for Joanna and me to become friends, I knew I needed a Christian friend, but I had no idea how to make it happen on my own. Similarly, many people feel a spiritual need, but without the guidance of the Holy Spirit, they can't figure out how to fill that need on their own.

Like Joanna coming to my table when I was feeling abandoned and thought I didn't want to talk to her, Jesus came to earth and died for us while we were lost and didn't know Him or even want to get to know Him.

My human logic said that Joanna was too popular and beautiful to want to be my friend. Human logic tells us that the idea of God becoming man and dying for our sins is too good to be true.

When Joanna came to my table, I could have just said hello, made a polite excuse, and left. I could have rejected the friendship she offered. That's what many people do with Jesus. They reject Jesus before they even know who He is.

It is such a relief to know that my salvation and the salvation of my family and friends is not up to me. I used to feel a lot of guilt and stress about not being effective enough in witnessing. I'm finally learning that although God wants me to share the truth about Jesus as best I can, He can help people know Him both with my help and despite my mess-ups. He gives me the honor of helping a little, but He doesn't need my help. He was making His salvation known for thousands of years before I was born and will continue to use His elaborate plans to reveal Himself until Jesus returns.

But do not overlook this one fact, beloved, that with the Lord one day is as a thousand years, and a thousand years as one day. The Lord is not slow to fulfill His promise as some count

Heather

187

slowness, but is patient toward you, not wishing that any should perish, but that all should reach repentance. 2 Peter 3:8–9

"For I know the plans I have for you," declares the Lord, "plans for welfare and not for evil, to give you a future and a hope." Jeremiah 29:11

Think about how God revealed Himself to you. Did His plan involve your parents bringing you to the font to be baptized as an infant and raising you to know Jesus, or did He introduce Himself to you later in life when you heard the Gospel? Get together with a Christian friend and share your salvation stories. Talk about how God planned and arranged for you to know Him and each other.

Prayer: Dear heavenly Father, thank You for revealing Yourself to me through Your Word! Thank You for Your Holy Spirit, who draws me to Your Word. Thank You for the people You have sent into my life to help me know You better. Thank You that You are in control and that You have chosen me to belong to You. Amen.

tuesday

Personal Study Questions:
Psalm 98:2

1. Today's faith narrative comments, "The whole Bible, both Old Testament and New Testament, work together as one story of how God carried out His plan to save us from our sins and reveal that plan of salvation to us." As the psalmist says in Psalm 98:2, "The LORD has made His salvation known."

   a. How did the Lord first make known His salvation to you?

   b. How has He made it known across the world?

   c. How does He continue to make it known to His people?

2. The righteousness of Christ Jesus now belongs to you. Jesus won this right-standing with God for you on Calvary's cross. You are "all right" with God. He considers you blameless and holy—just like Jesus. What "new song" does this truth bring to your heart?

Heather

Psalm 98:3

He has remembered His steadfast love and faithfulness to the house of Israel. All the ends of the earth have seen the salvation of our God.

God Remembers

Have you ever felt forgotten by God? Sometimes when people face tragedies, illnesses, and losses, they think God has forgotten them. They may feel like they have fallen off God's radar screen or wonder if He's stopped caring about them. Even Jesus felt that way when He was hanging on the cross and called out, "My God, My God, why have You forsaken Me?" (Matthew 27:46). Although Jesus knew exactly what God's plan was and He had chosen to carry it

190

out, as a human being, He still felt forgotten.

Last year, my husband and I went through a series of challenges that made us feel like God had forgotten us. It all started around our anniversary. We hadn't been getting along well and were hoping that a vacation would help us to reconnect and have time to talk through some problems. The trip started out on the right foot. We had lots of family time with our two-year-old son and were finally talking through a lot of issues that had been bothering us. But about halfway through our trip, we got an emergency call from my husband's parents. Our house had flooded. We had more than 6 feet of water in the basement, and about half of the main floor was damaged. As we drove home, I felt that same kind of numbness I felt when people who were really close to me had died. I kept remembering all the things that had been in the basement—diaries, photo albums, yearbooks, Christmas ornaments, keepsakes, almost all my books, and my wedding dress. Even worse than the grief over the losses was the idea of how much work it was going to be to clean up such a huge mess.

The clean up and repair process took even longer than I'd expected. For two months, we lived in a 20-foot camp trailer—with our potty-training-in-process son—while the house was being repaired and we sorted through the mess. I thought often of the people in New Orleans after Hurricane Katrina, where whole neighborhoods were a soggy muck and they didn't have cleanup crews available to help, stores to go to, or even a clean trailer to stay in. I tried to comfort myself with the thought that things could be worse.

Things did get worse. I got a bad cut on my foot and spent weeks limping through the mess as I cleaned and sorted. At the same time, my husband was having health problems, and we were fitting in visits to specialists among appointments with contractors and trips to buy renovation supplies. Then, I caught a really nasty stomach virus that made me so sick I could hardly get out of bed for a week.

We were finally able to move back into the house right before my husband started harvest. A few days after getting back

Heather

into the house, I was finally feeling like things were getting back to normal when I looked out the window and saw black smoke coming out from under the hood of our wheat truck. The fire was frightening enough, but it was parked only a few feet from our main farm shops where we store our equipment, vehicles, and tools. My husband ran to put out the fire and managed to get it out before it spread to the shops, but the truck was so badly damaged that he and his brother had to harvest without it that year.

Even at our very lowest points, when we felt forgotten, we knew God had not really forgotten us. We knew that God was loving us and remembering us every second of our struggle, just as He had remembered and cared for the Israelites while they wandered in the desert and the disciples while they were being persecuted.

In addition to the flood, fire, and harvest, we were also dealing with my husband's uncle having terminal cancer. My husband and his Uncle John were really close, and we were torn between wanting to spend time with him before he died and needing to get our home and health under control while my husband was working ridiculously long hours on the farm.

That fall, I got pregnant and was starting to feel hopeful and happy again. I felt like God was finally done with whatever lessons He was trying to teach us and we were going to get to enjoy some blessings for a change. But only weeks later, my husband's uncle passed away, and I miscarried our baby. While healing from the miscarriage and grieving for our baby and Uncle John, it became almost impossible for me to cope with sorting through the last of our damaged photos and keepsakes. For the next few months, the stress and sorrow became almost paralyzing. I became obsessively furious that my son's keepsake Christmas ornaments had made it safely through the flood only to be lost by the cleaning company who refused to even acknowledge or apologize for their negligence. I felt guilty that I was letting my son watch way too many videos because I just didn't have the energy to play with him. I grieved all the playtime and peaceful childhood memories he had lost during our move out of the house and then back into it after the repairs. I was discouraged that he had turned three and didn't seem

Heather

to be making progress toward being potty trained. My hair even started falling out. I knew that God never lets us be tempted beyond what we can bear, but I desperately wished He'd have a little less faith in my ability to cope.

Thankfully, my husband and I were raised knowing that we are saved by God's grace through faith. We knew that the only thing that really mattered was that Jesus had chosen us to belong to Him and that we were forgiven and would go to heaven some day. Even at our very lowest points, when we felt forgotten, we knew God had not really forgotten us. We knew that God was loving us and remembering us every second of our struggle, just as He had remembered and cared for the Israelites while they wandered in the desert and the disciples while they were being persecuted. We stubbornly clung to God just as He was clinging to us and sending us love and encouragement through the Bible:

But we have this treasure in jars of clay to show that the surpassing power belongs to God and not to us. We are afflicted in every way, but not crushed; perplexed, but not driven to despair; persecuted, but not forsaken; struck down, but not destroyed. 2 Corinthians 4:7–9

More than that, we also rejoice in our sufferings, knowing that suffering produces endurance, and endurance produces character, and character produces hope, and hope does not put us to shame, because God's love has been poured into our hearts through the Holy Spirit who has been given to us. Romans 5:3–5

Now, more than a year after our house flooded, I can even thank God for the difficult times, knowing that He caused incredible good to come out of the suffering. Because of all the troubles last year, my husband and I have a stronger faith and a much stronger marriage. Even more important, because Jeff's uncle knew he was dying ahead of time, he had time to finally sort out his beliefs and feelings about God. After more than sixty years of struggling with God, he was baptized only months before he died.

And we know that for those who love God all things work together for good, for those who are called according to His purpose. Romans 8:28

God has remembered His love and His faithfulness to the house of Israel, to me, and to you. I hope you never have to go through a year like we did. But if for some reason God allows a tragedy into your life, please always remember God never forgets.

Think about the three worst things that have happened to you, and look for what good God has done in your life because of those things. God never forgets His love; His salvation extends to all the ends of the earth.

Prayer: Dear heavenly Father, thank You for all of Your love and promises. Thank You that You always remember me. Please help me to cling to You when life gets hard, to see Your will in both good things and bad, and to always remember Your most important promise that all who believe and are baptized will be saved. In Jesus' name. *Amen.*

Heather

194

wednesday

Personal Study Questions: Psalm 98:3

1. God always remembers His "steadfast love and faithfulness." Take some time right now to do the same. What evidence of your Savior's steadfast love, of His faithfulness, can you recall . . .

   a. from your childhood?

   b. from your teen years?

   c. in each decade of your life since then?

2. The author of today's faith narrative invites us to "Think about the three worst things that have happened to you, and look for what good God has done in your life because of those things." If you could sit and talk with the author about this, what would you say?

3. The psalmist encourages us to remember that "All the ends of the earth have seen the salvation of our God." For which nations and people seemingly at the "ends of the earth" will you pray today?

4. What will you ask concerning the spread of the message of forgiveness and hope in Jesus? Jot some notes before you begin to pray. If you need help, think about recent news stories that demonstrate a need or a fresh opportunity for the Gospel message to work its way through a particular group or culture.

Heather

Psalm 98:4–6

Make a joyful noise to the LORD, all the earth; break forth into joyous song and sing praises! Sing praises to the LORD with the lyre, with the lyre and the sound of melody! With trumpets and the sound of the horn make a joyful noise before the King, the LORD!

A Joyful Noise

Music is a huge part of our worship at church. While sitting or standing among our brothers and sisters in Christ, it doesn't take long to realize that God has given different musical gifts and abilities to each of us. Some people sing with voices that sound like they've been professionally trained, others struggle to reach any recognizable note at all, and still others make up perhaps the largest group of singers, whether inside the church or out: those who are average.

Heather

For many of us, music is also a huge part of our personal worship outside of church. As a child, I felt that only praying, doing devotions, or reading my Bible counted as worshiping God at home. The problem was that all of those things seemed very formal, and I found it hard to make myself sit still to do them. I often talked to God during the day, but I didn't realize that those little chats counted as prayer just as much as when I sat down and said the Lord's Prayer. I felt closest to God when I was listened to Christian music and sang Christian songs around the house. Eventually, I realized that these times when I listened to or sang songs about God's love for us and our love for Him was also worship. The older I get, the more I learn about God's gift of music.

I've learned that music can touch emotions more deeply than words or thoughts alone can. When I got married, a good friend of my husband's sang "The Lord's Prayer" as a solo while we were standing in front of the altar. God has given this friend an amazingly strong and beautiful voice. The prayer somehow sounded even more like a prayer than usual. That was the point in the wedding when I couldn't stop myself from crying. Getting married was emotional enough, but praying the prayer Jesus gave us along with my new husband and all of the friends and family behind us while our friend was singing it so beautifully was more than my heart could hold. I felt it was a preview of when we would be in heaven someday in the presence of God with angels and believers praising Him.

I've learned that love songs aren't just for people. When I was single, for what seemed like forever, I was frustrated by how many of the songs on the radio were about romantic love. One day, I realized that some of those songs could be applied to our relationship with Jesus too. It was comforting to know that although I didn't have a man in my life who felt that way about me, Jesus and I had a loving relationship. I enjoyed belting out the songs to Jesus while waiting in traffic or cleaning house. I started to see personal worship as less formal. Since I didn't have dates most weekends, I started making dates with Jesus for Friday or Saturday night. I'd choose a small book of the Bible, read the

Heather

whole thing in one sitting, and then pray a little and sing a little.

I've learned that a song doesn't have to be well written to be meaningful. At different times in my life, I've chosen different songs as themes of self-expression. Sometimes, at really emotional times in my life, I couldn't think of a song with just the right lyrics to let out how I was feeling. At those times, I created songs by adding my own lyrics to familiar tunes. Sometimes I needed a new song. One summer while I was in university, I worked at a bridal shop. I spent most of the hot summer in the back room steaming dresses. Without having anyone to talk to all day, my mind wandered to feeling sorry for myself that all these dresses were for other women who were getting married and that I couldn't even get a date. The lyrics of the theme song I created for myself that summer were "I hate my job, I hate my life, I have no money, I'll never be a wife." Although the lyrics were negative, the cheerful tune I chose to sing them to took the sting out of their meaning. I sang them to the tune of the Pinocchio song "I've Got No Strings." The song reminded me that I wasn't really tied to any of the problems. I could quit the job if I wanted to. I didn't really hate my life; I was just very uncomfortable with several aspects of it at that time. Having no extra money was my choice. I purposely put it all into tuition and books so I wouldn't have to have crummy jobs forever. And only God knew when or if He would make me a wife. Although it had very basic lyrics and used a borrowed tune, the song did the job I needed it to do.

Today's Bible passage gives lots of options and doesn't say anything about skill. The point of the verse is to experience the joy of being saved by God and to express it with music.

I've learned that people of all ages can use music to express themselves. My three-year-old son uses songs to express great joy or pride, like when he finally used the potty. He didn't have a song with appropriate lyrics for such an occasion, so he just sang the ABC song at the top of his lungs. When he can't think of a song to get the emotions out, he just yells, "Honk!" His honk reminds me of the times when the Bible says, "Shout for joy." Music is so powerful for him that he often can't hold it inside. I've also seen how powerful music can be for elderly people who are coping

Heather

with memory loss. I've seen people who couldn't create a coherent sentence on their own anymore recognize or even sing a hymn or Sunday School song and feel comforted by it. The hymns and Bible verses they'd memorized as children decades earlier were little gems of comfort and worship when their minds no longer co-operated with them.

I've learned that God doesn't judge the quality of our music like we do. I love to sing, but my voice often doesn't match what my ears want to hear. Other people may notice my lack of talent, but God doesn't. Much like I love my preschooler's artwork even though it looks like scribbles to most people, God loves my attempts at singing to Him as if I were an award-winning musician.

I love that today's Bible passage gives lots of options and doesn't say anything about skill. The point of the verse is to experience the joy of being saved by God and to express it with music. We're told to shout, sing, or play an instrument. No matter what skills we have, all of us can do at least one of these things. I'm guessing that a blast of the ram's horn would sound a lot like my son's honk.

Take some time today to make a joyful noise to God. Either alone or with your family, express your joy to God with sound. You could choose a song to sing, blow party horns, play kazoos, or even just shout a phrase such as "Praise God!" The Lord deserves our jubilant song, no matter how it sounds. He has rescued us from our sins, and the life we have with Him we will enjoy forever.

Heather

199

Prayer: Thank You, Lord God, for the gift of my senses. In this world that can often feel too full of noise or too quiet, please help me to take time to regularly express my love for You with jubilant song. Thank You for Your gracious presence in the Gospel, in Baptism, in Absolution, and in Holy Communion. Help me to share Your love as I hug someone, speak kind words to them, or perform music that glorifies Your holy name. In Jesus' name. Amen.

Heather

Personal Study Questions:
Psalm 98:4–6

1 The psalmist names many instruments that in combination will "make a joyful noise." Which contemporary instruments would you suggest adding to this list?

2. Imagine instruments, both ancient and contemporary, combining with the voices of believers of all time and every place. How do you imagine that "noise" would sound? Which words would you personally add to the praises if you were to join that choir?

3. If time will allow, read the hymns of praise from Revelation 4:11; 5:9–10; and 5:12–13. What further ideas for your own hymn of praise do these verses add?

Heather

Psalm 98:7–9

Let the sea roar, and all that fills it, the world and those who dwell in it. Let the rivers clap their hands; let the hills sing for joy together before the LORD, for He comes to judge the earth. He will judge the world with righteousness and the people with equity.

Fair Judgment

When you hear the words *judge* or *judgment*, how do you feel? For most people, these words bring up emotions like fear or anger. In a courtroom, a judgment can lead to fines or jail time. In a schoolyard, the judgment of a popular student can make you either popular or a social outcast. It is often hard for people to understand God being both a loving God and our judge.

Our world is full of judgment and criticism. When I go through the checkout line with my groceries, I see mag-

Heather

202

azine covers with a variety of judgments about celebrities all over them. The magazines show unflattering photos of people and present stories about things like who has the best and worst beach body and who they think has had plastic surgery. When I look for a television show to watch, I have a hard time finding anything positive. The news shows, talk shows, situation comedies, and gossip shows are full of judgments based on worldly qualities like wealth, popularity, weight, and beauty. Even at church and among family members, I hear people gossiping about one another and judging others. One woman I know once admitted to me that she criticizes other people because it makes her feel better about herself.

Although being judged based on worldly values, like my weight, can hurt, it never hurts as much as being judged based on God's values. If someone says I'm fat, I know they're right but that my extra pounds have no eternal relevance. The size of clothes I wear doesn't matter to God. In fact, I've sometimes felt that my weight problem is kind of like the thorn in the flesh Paul talks about in the Bible. What the world sees as my faults may be God's way of keeping me from becoming vain or proud. I wonder if maybe God purposely created me with genes that hold onto fat cells because I can serve Him better this way. Struggling with my weight has made me more compassionate and less intimidating to others.

While I know that I am daily judged according to the world's standards, I'm not aware of being judged based on God's standards very often. One time I felt under a spiritual microscope was when I was doing my director of Christian education internship. Everyone there was extremely welcoming and loving. I felt an overwhelming desire and responsibility to do the very best I could to serve that congregation while I was there. Most of the congregation members welcomed me with an assumption that I knew what I was doing unless I proved otherwise. But there were a few people who weren't willing to trust me until they'd observed me for a while. They were polite and fairly friendly, but I could feel them holding back a part of themselves until they were sure I'd

Heather

proven myself.

I had an amazing youth group at that church. Several of them had an intensity and maturity of faith I had never seen before in anyone so young. One of the boys, in particular, stands out in my memory. He was one of the oldest in the youth group and had taken upon himself the role of protector. Each week, as I presented a new Bible study, he would scrutinize everything I said to make sure that what I taught was doctrinally sound. He would ask very advanced questions and watch me with a serious face as he judged whether my answer fit with what he knew about the Bible and doctrine. I was proud of him for being so responsible, knowledgeable, and protective of the group; but I was also a little hurt that this kid, who was ten years younger than me, was taking so long to trust me. I'd been a Christian my whole life, been trained as a director of Christian education at a Lutheran college, and been placed at that church as an intern by the mutual agreement of the director of my program and the congregation. While I admired his strength of character, it seemed ridiculous that this teenager felt he needed to challenge what dozens of adults had decided was God's will.

I'm not afraid to die, and I'm not afraid of Jesus' returning because I know I am saved by grace through faith. God's judgment doesn't scare me because I know that although I can never perfectly keep His Law, He has sent His Son, Jesus, to keep it in my place and to die for me and save me from my sins.

While kids in other youth groups I'd led may have judged me based on my weight, hairstyle, car, or clothes, this young man was measuring my teaching against God's Word. I had always been able to handle judgments based on worldly things, such as my appearance or bank account, but it really bothered me to have someone questioning whether I was being true to God's Word. I was becoming increasingly nervous about youth nights because I felt such pressure to make sure that the Bible studies were presented so everyone could get something out of them, whether they were visitors who knew very little about Jesus or were one of the teens who knew their Bibles better than many adults.

One week, I chose a topic that I knew would get everyone

Heather

thinking. The title of our study was "Is God Fair?" I knew I was taking an unusual angle on the answer, and I expected that the topic would generate lots of conversation and be a great way to get the group talking about how our salvation is a free gift from God. What I didn't see coming was how concerned the topic would make the young man who watched to see that I stayed true to God's Word and presented correct doctrine. He and the group all expected me to tell them that God is fair, but I suggested that God is not fair. I immediately had everyone's undivided attention. Several of the group members looked concerned, and this boy looked horrified. I'm sure he considered running out of the room to find our pastor. I explained to the group that in one sense, God is very fair. He doesn't discriminate based on gender, age, wealth, popularity, or beauty. As today's Bible passage tells us, He judges with equity. But we can also say that God isn't fair because we don't get what we deserve. The Bible tells us that "the wages of sin is death" (Romans 6:23). According to the Law, it is not fair for us to be forgiven or saved. The fair consequence of our sinfulness is for us to be separated from God forever. It wasn't fair for Jesus to have to die in our place. The amazing thing about Christianity is that God, who is perfect and all-powerful, loves us so much that He chose mercy over fairness. He chose to send His only Son to take the consequences for our sins as a free gift to us rather than giving us what we deserve. "The wages of sin is death, but the free gift of God is eternal life" (Romans 6:23). That lesson was a turning point for the young man who was judging my teaching. After that day, I felt that he had learned to trust that I was doing my best to teach only what the Bible says. I'm proud to share that this same young man is all grown up now, and he and his wife are missionaries overseas.

There is a huge difference between people judging us based on worldly values and God judging us based on His holy Law. As a Christian, I know that I am sinful. I know that if God were to judge me based on my own actions and thoughts, I'd have no chance at all of getting to heaven. But I'm not afraid to die, and I'm not afraid of Jesus' returning because I know I am saved by

Heather

grace through faith. God's judgment doesn't scare me because I know that although I can never perfectly keep His Law, He has sent His Son, Jesus, to keep it in my place and to die for me and save me from my sins.

Make a list of worldly judgments people have made about you, and then destroy the list to remind yourself that those judgments will pass away with this world. Only how God sees you matters for eternity. God has judged you on the basis of Christ's righteousness, and you are holy and wholly His through His saving name.

Prayer: Dear Father in heaven, thank You for loving me just the way I am. When I start to feel crushed by the world's judgments, please help me to remember how You see me, Lord. Please help me to ignore judgments based on the world's values and to focus on what You want for my life. In Jesus' name. Amen.

Heather

Personal Study Questions:
Psalm 98:7–9

1. In today's faith narrative, the author shares several examples of judgment by others that hurt her or created anxiety in her heart. When have things like that happened to you?

2. God comes to judge (v. 9), yet all creation praises and all believers ("the righteous") rejoice. How can judgment provoke praise? (See vv. 1–3.)

3. In the concluding verses of Psalm 98, all nature joins in the mighty roar of praise begun in the earlier verses assigned for yesterday. What additional pictures and words of joy and wonder do the concluding verses of the psalm suggest?

Heather

Group Bible Study for Week 6
Psalm 98

1. Psalm 98 is yet another psalm that points forward to the Messiah, the world's Savior promised by God to His covenant people for centuries.

   a. Where do you see the work of that Savior foreshadowed in the psalm?

   b. Which promises and word pictures portraying the promised Savior and His work particularly thrilled you as you read and pondered them in the psalm this past week?

   c. Which examples and other content from the week's faith narratives particularly encouraged you?

   d. Which promises in the psalm have already been fulfilled? Which remain to be fulfilled?

   e. What joys, hopes, fears, questions, or concerns does all this evoke in your heart?

2. Psalm 98 definitely fits in the "messianic" category. Why? It also fits in the "missional" category. Why?

3. Psalm 98 lifts crescendos of praise to our Savior-God. Share with the members of your group the thoughts and prayers of praise and worship this psalm drew from your heart as you studied it this week, particularly on Thursday and Friday.

4. If we would receive from a holy God what we justly deserve in the Day of Judgment, we would surely shrink in terror (v. 9). Yet the psalmist encourages us to join the hills and rivers in clapping our hands and singing for joy. Verses 1–3 tell us what makes this possible.

a. Explain your reasons for joy in the judgment.

b. This joy comes to us only in Jesus, our King, the Lord (v. 6). How does Acts 4:12 express this truth?

c. How would you respond to someone who rejected this exclusive claim of Christianity by saying something like "I can't believe God is that narrow or mean-spirited. I try my best to love, to live and let live. I'm sure that's good enough. God *is* love, after all. And nobody's perfect!"

5. All the psalms in this volume of A New Song focus on King Jesus, who is anointed and reigning on Zion's holy hill. God could have chosen Babylon with its hanging gardens and other architectural achievements as the throne for the Messiah. He could have chosen Alexandria with its famous library and other intellectual accomplishments. Instead, He chose Zion, a smallish hill in a dusty land, as His Son's throne. Today, that Son lives in humble human hearts—yours and mine. What does this tell you about His grace, His mercy? (See 1 Corinthians 1:26–31 and the Introduction to this volume on p. 10.)

6. As you review each of the six psalms you have studied over the past several weeks (Psalms 2; 20; 21; 45; 72; and 98), what words of adoration, confession, thanksgiving, and supplication would you like to offer to your Savior-God, Zion's King?

Small-Group Leader Guide

This guide will help guide you in discovering the truths of God's Word. It is not, however, exhaustive, nor is it designed to be read aloud during your session.

1. Before you begin, spend some time in prayer, asking God to strengthen your faith through a study of His Word. The Scriptures were written so that we might believe in Jesus Christ and have life in His name (John 20:31). Also, pray for participants by name.

2. Before your meeting, review the session material, read the Bible passages, and answer the questions in the spaces provided. Your familiarity with the session will give you confidence as you lead the group.

3. As a courtesy to participants, begin and end each session on time.

4. Have a Bible dictionary or similar resource handy to look up difficult or unfamiliar names, words, and places. Ask participants to help you in this task. Be sure that each participant has a Bible and a study guide.

5. Ask for volunteers to read introductory paragraphs and Bible passages. A simple "thank you" will encourage them to volunteer again.

6. See your role as a conversation facilitator rather than a lecturer. Don't be afraid to give participants time to answer questions. By name, thank each participant who answers; then invite other input. For example, you may say, "Thank you, Maggie. Would anyone else like to share?"

7. Now and then, summarize aloud what the group has learned by studying God's Word.

8. Remember that the questions provided are discussion starters. Allow participants to ask questions that relate to the session. However, keep discussions on track with the session.

9. Everyone is a learner! If you don't know the answer to a question, simply tell participants that you need time to look at more Scripture passages or to ask your pastor.

Week 1, Psalm 2

Personal Study Questions

Monday—Psalm 2:1–3

1. The opening verses of Psalm 2 picture "the LORD" and "His anointed [the Messiah]" as reigning in heaven, noting the rebellion of the earth's sinful people. They rage against their rightful Ruler "in vain" because He is all-powerful. Still their rebellion continues because in their spiritually dead condition they hate God's rule, His authority over them.

2. Answers will vary. Evidence of continuing rebellion by our society today and of that rebellion in our own hearts will not be hard to find. This rightly terrifies us until we remember that our King is also our Savior. We have His promise: "If we confess our sins, [God] is faithful and just to forgive us our sins and to cleanse us from all unrighteousness" (1 John 1:8–9).

Tuesday—Psalm 2:4–6

1. The Lord laughs at the ravings of earth's puny rebels.

2. The Lord "set [His] King on Zion," declaring that King to be His representative. Neither God's Law nor His judgment on sinful people will change. Human beings will not be allowed to set their own agendas, to control their own lives. This terrifies those who hate and fear God's rule. They think all they want is for God to leave them alone, but in wanting that, they are in reality asking for hell itself—total separation from God and His love forever.

3. Answers will vary.

Wednesday—Psalm 2:7–9

1. The Father declares the Messiah to be His Son, His rightful heir and ruler over the earth, especially "Zion" (v. 6), His Church. The Father promises to hear His Son's request to give Him the nations, the ends of the earth as His inheritance. The Lord has answered that prayer in countless ways down

through the centuries since Christ's ascension. On the Day of Pentecost, for example, the Lord added three thousand believers to His Church; He continues to answer that prayer today as many come to the knowledge of the truth in Jesus, their Savior.

2. The Father promised to give the Son "the nations;" the Son commissioned His Church to "make disciples of all nations" by baptizing and teaching. By God's grace, we share the joy of extending the kingdom of grace across the world as we ourselves witness, as we send and support those in mission fields worldwide, and as we pray for the Spirit to work faith in hearts touched by the Gospel.

3. Answers will vary.

Thursday—Psalm 2:10–11

1. Answers will vary; arguably the verses describe all three. The Messiah is kind, true, and powerful, but we dare not try to manipulate or deceive Him. Wisdom bows before the all-wise, all-powerful King in honor, faith, and submission. Psalm 111:10 describes this same wise response.

2. The faith narrative focuses attention on what it means to "rejoice with trembling." Answers will vary.

Friday—Psalm 2:12

1. Answers will vary.

2. We read Law in the command that we submit to the rule of the Messiah in unconditional obedience to that rule. A lack of submission, the verse warns, will result in the Son's anger and in our perishing. The Gospel is the promise in the last sentence, "Blessed are all who take refuge in Him." We find refuge in the Son and in His cross from the punishment we rightly deserve for our sins. He Himself bore the punishment we earned by our rejection of His rule!

3. Answers will vary.

Group Bible Study for Week 1

1. Let volunteers share. Answers will vary.

2. The psalm text focuses two "cameras" on reality, so to speak—the reality in heaven and that on earth. Work together to make two lists describing events and attitudes found in each setting. We sometimes find ourselves among those trying to shake off God's rightful authority over us. But by grace, we also find ourselves in the last sentence of the psalm, taking refuge in Jesus.

3. Answers will vary.

4. If Christ is who Scripture says He is, then those in rebellion against His gracious rule are rightly terrified as they consider the Day of Judgment and His eternal rule. Answers will vary regarding evidence of this terror as portrayed in the media and elsewhere in our culture.

5. Answers will vary.

6. Answers will vary.

Week 2, Psalm 20

Personal Study Questions

Monday—Psalm 20:1–3

1. The faith narrative describes a series of serious personal health challenges the author experienced after a fall from a horse. The Gospel writers (Matthew, Mark, Luke, and John) describe many instances of opposition our Lord faced during His earthly life—criticism from authorities, doubt on the part of His followers and His own family, death threats from those in His hometown, and, ultimately, His suffering and crucifixion.

2. Answers will vary.

3. God's ultimate answer to Jesus' "day of trouble" was the resurrection. In it, Jesus conquered every enemy and cut off every objection to His teachings. Because of the resurrection, we can rely on God's constant care and help for us today, no matter what challenges we may face.

4. Answers will vary.

Tuesday—Psalm 20:4–5

1. Answers will vary.

2. The "offering" or "sacrifice" (verse 3) we especially want the Father to remember is that of Christ on Calvary. Since God gave us His best in giving us Jesus, we know for sure He will not withhold any other good thing we need. See Romans 8:32.

3. Answers will vary.

Wednesday—Psalm 20:6

1. Our "faith and hope are in God," as Peter tells us, because God raised Jesus from the dead. The resurrection proves that God accepted the Son's sacrifice for our sins. Through faith in the Messiah, God's "anointed one," we receive all the blessings Jesus earned for us in His Passion— forgiveness, life, peace, joy, the riches of heaven. All these and more besides are ours because Jesus died for us and rose again.

2. Answers will vary.

3. Answers will vary.

Thursday—Psalm 20:7–8

1. The "name" communicates the totality of who the Lord is for us. It contains in a kind of shorthand form all His promises to us and all His work for us. See Philippians 2:10.

2. God places His name upon His people through His "visible Word" in Holy Baptism. We are marked as belonging to Him. (See Revelation 7:3 and 14:1.)

3. Answers will vary.

Friday—Psalm 20:9

1. Answers will vary.

2. Answers will vary.

Group Bible Study for Week 2

1. Answers will vary.

2. Answers will vary.

3. Answers will vary.

4. Jesus gave Himself fully to the Lord on the tree of the cross, where He absorbed the curse of sin in our place. Now, we respond by giving ourselves totally back to Him—not necessarily in death, although many believers around the world do live in daily danger of martyrdom, but as we serve Him by serving other people in our day-to-day, moment-to-moment lives.

5. Answers will vary.

6. Answers will vary. Share your confidence in Jesus and your love for Him as you talk through these questions with one another.

Week 3, Psalm 21

Personal Study Questions

Monday—Psalm 21:1

1. Among other things, the author describes the ways she has depended on her earthly father for help throughout her growing up years and in the years following. She connects this with her reliance on God's willingness and ability to hear and respond to her requests for help.

2. Answers will vary.

3. Jesus' "heart's desire" was and is our salvation. God has granted this, and it brings Jesus great joy—not to mention the joy we ourselves experience. Using very little imagination, we can hear Jesus singing this psalm of praise to God as He enters heaven's courts, carrying the scars of victory in His hands, feet, and side as the angels bow in deep worship. See also Psalm 68:18.

Tuesday—Psalm 21:2–5

1. Answers will vary.

2. The crown in verse 3 signifies victory, power, rule, and authority.

3. Jesus asked the Father for life, and the Father granted it in the resurrection. This life will never end. As a beloved Easter hymn puts it, "He [Jesus] lives eternally to save" (*Lutheran Service Book* 461:2).

4. Answers will vary. Our very existence as the redeemed daughters of God honors the Messiah. See Ephesians 1:12 ("we . . . might *be* to the praise of His glory;" emphasis added).

Wednesday—Psalm 21:6–7

1. King David's just, forward-looking, and compassionate earthly rule certainly blessed the people of Israel. But more to the point, through David's descendents, God sent the world's Savior, the Messiah. Thus, David was a blessing forever and, living forever because of the redemption that Savior provided, David is also blessed forever. King Jesus brings eternal blessings to all who believe in Him; He is a blessing to us forever. He is also blessed/ honored eternally by the Father, the hosts of heaven, and by those whom He has redeemed—us.

2. Answers will vary.

3. The Lord brought David safely through many battles and on into the glories of heaven. David received these blessings through faith in the Messiah who was to come. The Lord brought His Messiah through many earthly dangers, protecting Him and keeping Him steadfast, immovable, as He earned salvation for us. Now, through faith, these words also describe us—His royal priests—as the Lord keeps us steadfast, immovable, for the work He has prepared for us to do. See 1 Corinthians 15:58.

Thursday—Psalm 21:8–12

1. Answers will vary.

2. Answers will vary. The psalmist's words will evoke many different insights.

3. We praise Jesus because of what He has done for us. No matter how talented we might be, musically or in any other way, our ability to honor Him pales when we consider the magnitude of the praise He deserves.

Friday—Psalm 21:13

1. Answers will vary.

2. As the Holy Spirit continues to teach us through His Word, our understanding of the Lord's glory grows. Our ability to comprehend and will-

ingness to trust His glorious work for us expands. In this way, He is "magnified" and "exalted."

Group Bible Study for Week 3

1. Answers will vary.

2. Let volunteers comment. At several points, the psalm describes King David's earthly rule.

3. Again, let volunteers comment. Read in the light of the New Testament, the psalm describes the work of the Messiah throughout.

4. Answers will vary; accept those that are reasonable in light of what Jesus has done for us in the redemption. In addition to Ephesians 1:3–14, 1 Peter 2:9–10 also helps apply the words of the psalm to us, Christ's redeemed.

5. The entire psalm describes the Messiah's glory. In John's Gospel, Jesus Himself describes that glory coming to Him as He is "lifted up." The psalm describes the Messiah's enemies and talks about the Messiah's trust in the Lord in the face of these enemies (v. 7). Unmoved by their opposition, the King wins the victory. All this hints at the fact that God knew from all eternity the resistance and hatred Jesus would one day endure. Yet, despite even the opposition of Satan himself, Jesus would win the victory. This victory made our salvation possible and brought Jesus great glory.

6. Read words and phrases from the texts themselves. If possible, use several Bible versions. Christ shares His glory with us, His people! Incredible!

7. Again, read specific phrases from the text, phrases that name and describe specific blessings. Here, Jesus prays for the unity of His Church. He asserts that He has given us the same glory the Father gave Him. He asks that that glory create our unity. Considering that Christ's glory was and is, in part, His service for us and considering the extreme love our Savior has for us (John 17:23) sheds additional light on the oneness for which Jesus prayed. The psalm foreshadows all this in several places, but especially in verse 5 as it describes the great glory belonging to the Messiah through the salvation He would earn for us.

Discuss the suitability of Psalm 21 as a hymn of praise in response to

Christ's work. Then pray the psalm together as you conclude today's session.

Week 4, Psalm 45

Personal Study Questions

Monday—Psalm 45:1–2

1. Answers will vary.
2. Answers will vary.
3. Answers will vary.
4. Jesus speaks words of forgiveness, peace, compassion, and help to all repentant sinners. How good for us to know this abundant grace!

Tuesday—Psalm 45:3–5

1. The language is very dramatic and paints pictures of powerful and heroic expeditions of rescue.
2. Answers will vary. The "sword" Jesus carries is His strong Word (Ephesians 6:17). As we saw in last week's study, the "splendor" and "majesty" (v. 4) that make Him glorious are His love for us and the suffering, death, and resurrection by which He won salvation for us. His throne is forever—His kingdom will have no end. Additional answers are possible.
3. Answers will vary.

Wednesday—Psalm 45:6–7

1. Answers will vary. Refer to today's faith narrative.
2. In verse 6, the psalmist calls the Messiah "God." The same verse refers to an eternal throne and to a scepter of uprightness or complete justice. This Ruler hates wickedness (v. 7) and rules in righteousness.
3. The phrase "oil of gladness," refers to the Holy Spirit.
4. Answers will vary.

Thursday—Psalm 45:8–12

1. Answers will vary. The psalm verses describe a powerful, wealthy, flourishing royal court. Note the details that are similar or identical in Psalm 45 and in Revelation 21:9–27.

2. Christ drapes His very own robe of righteousness around us, the robe He won for us at the cross.

3. Answers will vary.

4. Answers will vary. The faith narrative—and today's assigned verses from Psalm 45 as well—encourage us to see one another as fellow heirs of glory, guests all at the eternal wedding feast of our Savior.

Friday—Psalm 45:13–17

1. Right now, we belong to Christ. Right now, the King "desires our beauty" (v. 11). Right now, we can forget our former lives apart from Jesus and focus on the glorious inheritance we receive in Him. Right now, we wear the heavenly garments described in verse 14 and can rest in the joy and gladness that belong to us as God's adopted children. Ephesians 1:3–14 adds further details to our status right now as heaven's royal heirs.

In another sense, however, much glory still awaits us when Christ returns and we see Him with our physical eyes, walk heaven's streets in person, and enjoy blessings we cannot even imagine right now.

2. The Holy Spirit intends this metaphor, drawn from everyday life, to help us better grasp concepts that lie beyond our current, limited understanding.

3. Answers will vary.

Group Bible Study for Week 4

1. Share your thoughts and insights with one another. Many answers are possible.

2. Psalm 45 includes many details appropriate for a love song. As the psalm begins, it seems that God's people may be singing these words to our Messiah, our Savior-King, but especially toward the end of the psalm

(vv. 16–17), it becomes obvious that this love song originates within the Godhead. The Father and the Holy Spirit sing it to the Son, addressing some stanzas (e.g., v. 10) to us, members in Christ's Church.

We can, of course, incorporate some of these inspired words into our own hymns and songs of praise. The verses from Zephaniah referenced here describe Jesus singing love songs over us! Taken together, all this paints a beautiful picture of mutual love and devotion between God and His people.

3. Answers will vary.

4. Answers will vary.

5. Both Psalm 2:8 and Psalm 45:17 include the Lord's promise to extend the fame, authority, and honor of the Messiah throughout every time and place. Incredibly, God intends to use our witness as the means by which He fulfills that promise!

6. The words of Psalm 45 do describe Jesus' tender love. He showed His meekness (v. 4) in submitting to death to win our salvation. However, He is anything but "mild" in His defense of us engendered by His fierce love for us and His commitment to us. Let volunteers suggest appropriate hymns of worship.

7. Answers will vary. Incorporate as much of this conversation as possible into your closing prayer time.

Week 5, Psalm 72

Personal Study Questions

Monday—Psalm 72:1–7

1. Answers will vary.

2. Answers will vary.

3. Answers will vary.

4. Verses 1–7 include a rich description of the Messiah's eternal deliverance and righteous rule. For example, He is glad to "defend the cause of the poor," "give deliverance to the needy," and "crush the oppressor." What a description of the Messiah meeting the desperate needs of those oppressed by

Satan in our sin, guilt, and spiritual poverty! How we need the peace (v. 7) His atonement brings. Many additional insights may be drawn.

Tuesday—Psalm 72:8–11

1. From verse 8 onward, the descriptions of the Messiah become even more expansive. His rule extends to the ends of the earth. His name and fame continue forever. People are blessed in Him, and all nations call Him blessed (v. 17). These last words call to mind the messianic promise given to Abraham in Genesis 12:3 and 17:1–8. Other responses are possible.

2. See today's faith narrative. These verses are traditionally read at Epiphany; they prophesy the worship of the Christ child by the Magi and the extension of the "blessing of Abraham" to the Gentiles.

3. Answers will vary.

Wednesday—Psalm 72:12–14

1. Answers will vary. Earthly rulers are responsible, under God, to protect, in particular, their weakest and most helpless constituents. See Romans 13:1–7.

2. Compare these verses with Jesus' words in Luke 4:16–19. Those in need of pardon, those who recognize their spiritual poverty, those who understand themselves to be too weak to save themselves—Jesus came to rescue all of us from the oppression of sin and Satan, hell and death.

3. Answers will vary.

Thursday—Psalm 72:15–17

1. Verse 17 notes explicitly that the name of the Messiah endures forever. The people are "blessed in Him" (v. 17) and pray for Him (v. 15) all day long. They "blossom in the cities" (v. 16). Other phrases may also be appropriately cited.

2. No human being could possibly fit the description of super-human goodness, justice, and power described in Psalm 72. Only Jesus can and does fit the descriptions the psalm presents.

3. Answers will vary.

Friday—Psalm 72:18–20

1. Answers will vary.
2. Answers will vary.

Group Bible Study for Week 5

1. Answers will vary.
2. Participants may cite any of many verses from Psalm 72.
3. Answers will vary. Throughout the entire Scripture, the Holy Spirit urges God's people to care for the poor and oppressed. God hears the cry of the needy and has compassion on them. Likewise, He expects us as His children to care for the poor in a similar way. How might your congregation or small group respond more vigorously and in a timely way to the needs around you?
4. Invite volunteers to speculate. Answers will vary.
5. Answers will vary.
6. Let individuals comment. Then incorporate verses 18–19 into today's closing prayer.

Week 6, Psalm 98

Personal Study Questions

Monday—Psalm 98:1

1. Answers will vary.
2. Beginning with forgiveness of sins, God's gift of salvation includes innumerable, priceless blessings. Name as many as you can.

Tuesday—Psalm 98:2

1. Answers will vary.

2. Answers will vary.

Wednesday—Psalm 98:3

1. Answers will vary.

2. Answers will vary.

3. For more ideas, you may also want to check out this Web site: www.lcms.org/pages/internal.asp?NavID=4861.

4. Answers will vary.

Thursday—Psalm 98:4–6

1. Answers will vary.

2. Answers will vary.

3. Answers will vary.

Friday—Psalm 98:7–9

1. Answers will vary.

2. A sense of justice is built into God's creation. Children in kindergarten often complain, "It's not fair!" Although an objective assessment of our own situation before God should lead us to cry out for mercy, rather than justice, we still want to believe that God "balances the books" at some point. This "balancing" (and even the hope it will someday happen) leads us to praise a holy and just Creator.

3. Answers will vary.

Group Bible Study for Week 6

1. Several verses of the psalm transparently predict the work and glory of the coming Messiah. Let volunteers share their thoughts. See especially verses 2–3 and 8–9 as you consider the work Christ has already accomplished and work yet to be done.

2. Let participants offer evidence. Verses 3, 4, and 7 are transparently missional in referring to the spread of the Gospel to the ends of the earth.

Some participants may also mention verse 9; in light of the coming righteous judgment, how necessary it is that we proclaim to those who do not yet know it, the righteousness Christ won for us on Calvary's cross.

3. Answers will vary.

4. Answers will vary. As the group focuses on the question of how to address the challenge that Christianity's exclusive claims are "too narrow" and that God ought to accept each person's "best efforts," first address the fact that Jesus Himself claimed to be the only way to the Father (e.g., John 14:6; Acts 4:12). Additionally, Christianity is not the only faith system that claims its approach alone results in salvation. Most other world religions make similar assertions. These claims cannot all be true, so the question becomes, "Are any of them true? And if so, which ones?"

The Christian Scriptures assert that a just and holy God must and will punish sin. What would we think of an earthly judge who let offenders go free, defending the injustice by saying, "They did their best"? God's Law comes without loopholes. It does not say "try hard;" the Law says, "Do this, and you will live!" (Luke 10:28). Jesus Himself testifies to this. Failure to "do" makes those who disobey worthy of eternal death.

Scripture also testifies to the fact that all human beings have rebelled against God's righteous rule. We have disobeyed. We have all "gone astray" (Isaiah 53:6; Romans 3:9–18). But while we wallowed in the quicksand of our own guilt, God provided certain rescue in Jesus' death and resurrection. He offers it freely to all. This plan of salvation satisfied the claims of justice, while at the same time providing rescue for fallen humanity. God is both "just and the justifier of the one who has faith in Jesus" (Romans 3:26).

Interested participants may want to explore this key Christian teaching further by reading *Worldviews: A Christian Response to Religious Pluralism* by Anthony J. Steinbronn. This volume is available from CPH (item number 12-4211).

5. The passage cited from 1 Corinthians 1:26–31 helps to answer the first question in this section. God's mercy does not come to us because of our great intellect, our wonderful talents, our malleable hearts, or for any other reason resident in us. Rather, it comes to us simply because of our need. God had mercy on us in our need because He is gracious!

Base your closing prayer on the comments participants make as they review the six psalms in this six-week study (Psalms 2; 20; 21; 45; 72; and 98).